PRAISE FOR

Stop Saying You're Fine

"Mel Robbins is one of the most entertaining and compelling voices today. Read at your own risk. Mel will obliterate your excuses and leave you inspired, empowered, and on fire."

—DARREN HARDY, publisher of *Success* magazine
and bestselling author of *The Compound Effect*

"Mel Robbins has the guts to tell you why your brain is your biggest problem—but only if you listen to it. Here, she tells you how to power through and get what you want. I, for one, am listening."

—CHRIS BROGAN, president of Human
Business Works and coauthor of the
New York Times bestseller *Trust Agents*

"In *Stop Saying You're Fine*, Mel Robbins draws on everything from cutting-edge research to countless real-world case studies to create a wonderful program for anyone who's ever wanted to stop wishing and start doing."

—MARCI SHIMOFF, author of the *New York
Times* bestsellers *Love for No Reason* and
Happy for No Reason

"Quit whining, stop saying you're fine, and just snap out of it. Easier said than done, of course, which is why this road map is so remarkable. It's jam-packed with concrete steps to pave the way."

—TORY JOHNSON, workplace contributor for *Good
Morning America* and CEO of Women For Hire

"*Stop Saying You're Fine* nails a national problem: our tendency to try and be strong and stay the course—when it's the course we have to change, and strength is not working in our favor! In this no-nonsense book, every page demolishes the excuses we all make for not moving ahead with our lives, and gives us solid practical assignments that help us be better, happier, and more fulfilled. Robbins is wonderfully inspiring and helpful, but also hugely entertaining—moving forward doesn't have to be dull or depressing! You'll be surprised how her small suggestions can create life-changing new directions. *Stop Saying You're Fine* deserves to be a bestseller."

—PEPPER SCHWARTZ, PH.D., professor of
sociology, University of Washington, and
author of *Prime: Adventures and Advice on
Sex, Love, and the Sensual Years*

Stop Saying You're Fine

The No-BS Guide to *Getting What You Want*

Mel Robbins

Three Rivers Press
New York

Originally published in hardcover in the United States
by Crown Archetype, an imprint of the Crown Publishing Group,
a division of Random House, Inc., New York, in 2011.

Library of Congress Cataloging-in-Publication Data
is available upon request.

ISBN 978-0-307-71673-6
eISBN 978-0-307-71674-3

Printed in the United States of America

BOOK DESIGN BY BARBARA STURMAN
COVER PHOTOGRAPH: © MELISSA MAHONEY

20 19 18 17 16 15 14

First Paperback Edition

I wrote this *for you.*

CONTENTS

Stop Saying
You're Fine

It's not because things are difficult that we don't dare.
It's because we don't dare that things are difficult.

—SENECA
(Roman philosopher, 1st century A.D.)

INTRODUCTION

Every day you're bombarded with images of people doing better than you. There is an endless stream of reality shows selling the fantasy that somewhere out there are celebrity trainers, designers, and talent scouts helping people just like you lose weight, spice up their wardrobes, or launch music careers. Hollywood cranks out movie after movie about "ordinary people" who are impossibly sexy, funny, and adventurous. Log onto Facebook, and it seems as if everyone but you spends all his or her time having fun.

Of course, you know this isn't how the world actually works. There's no reality-show fairy godmother coming to whisk you away to a magical life. You don't have an entire Hollywood makeup team helping you look good, or screenwriters coming up with adventures to spice up your day. Facebook is nothing but heavily packaged "Kodak moments" that bear no relation to how people really live.

But even though you know all of these things are fake, there's still a part of you that wonders why your life isn't more satisfying.

You know life isn't a movie, but does it have to be so boring? Does it have to require so much effort? It's not that things are awful, they just . . . aren't that great. You say you're "fine," but you want more from life. The gap between the life you secretly *wish* you could lead and the life you're leading seems to be growing every day. This is your reality.

But it doesn't have to be.

In fact, the truth is that at this very moment, you couldn't *buy* better odds for success.

Everything you need to get whatever you want is there for the taking. There's a step-by-step instruction book for any subject, written by a fully credentialed expert. There are millions of blogs to walk you through any conceivable lifestyle change. There is free technology available to help you launch a business, sell your stuff, or publish your ideas. There are a thousand different networking tools to help you make new friends or find true love.

No, you don't have a reality show or Hollywood team doing everything for you—but you don't need them. **You are very powerful when you put your mind to it.** Everything you could ever need to live the life you want is right there at your fingertips. If you feel bored or stuck, it isn't because of the economy, or a lack of resources, or because America hasn't voted you its next idol. The real reason you feel stuck is you.

You are in your own way. If you don't feel like it, you don't do it. If you think you can't, you won't. If you can avoid confrontation or challenge, you do. If you can figure out a way to do nothing, you will. Your feelings are in charge of your head and they are running you into the ground. It is you who are robbing yourself of power and happiness.

If you could get out of your own way, you could have everything you want. You could be healthier. You could be more confident. You could be more successful. You could be happier. You could be more powerful. You could shrink that gap between the life you want and the life you lead, until it doesn't exist at all.

This book will teach you how.

Part I: *Why You Aren't Getting What You Want*

Given the choice between accomplishing something and just lying around, I'd rather lie around.
No contest.

—ERIC CLAPTON

CHAPTER ONE

Stop Hitting the Snooze Button

There are some days when you just feel more powerful. You force yourself to get up early and break a sweat before everyone else wakes up. That sets the tone for the rest of your day. Your coffee tastes especially good, and the commute doesn't suck. At work, you go the extra mile on a project and come off looking like a hero. Afterward, you meet some friends whom you haven't seen in months, and have a couple of drinks on an outdoor deck in the cool summertime air. Someone hands you tickets he couldn't use. You embrace spontaneity and go see a great show. Afterward, you drive home by moonlight, have great sex, and drift off to sleep on a cloud.

We've all had days when we feel excited about our lives. We feel young, confident, and alive. Everything clicks. We feel like we're going somewhere, like we have momentum. We become more powerful versions of ourselves.

The powerful you is always there waiting, like a switch inside you that needs to be turned on! It's the part of you that loves discovery, curiosity, challenges, exercise, connecting with other people, checking off goals, taking action, heading somewhere, and talking out loud. It is a force inside you that wants to grow, move, and expand. All you have to do is locate the switch and turn it on.

At the same time, there's an equal and opposite force that works inside you to hold you back. You were born with *resistance*. It's an inner, evolutionary bias to take the safe bet, the sure thing, the known path. Whenever you're feeling bored, bummed, or broken, your power is off and resistance is on. Resistance loves surfing the Web, vegging out in front of the TV, sticking to routine, not picking up the phone, hitting snooze, avoiding confrontation, making excuses, rumination, and isolation.

Resistance will keep your life in place; the power inside you will push your life forward. You will always feel tension between these two forces. Every single day of your life, you have the choice to stay where you are or move your life in new directions. The question is: **Will the powerful you turn on and start taking action, or will you resist and wait just a little longer to get the joy, satisfaction, and fulfillment you deserve?**

The Snooze Button

Right now, resistance is winning. Just consider how you start each day. The alarm goes off and to your sleeping self the sound seems to start somewhere behind your eyeballs. You instantly press the snooze button. Silence returns and you consider your options. Today was supposed to be the fifth day of your new exercise program. But it feels awfully early to be getting out of bed and walking across the cold floor in your bare feet. The mere thought of it makes your head throb.

You think about that calendar on the closet wall where you stuck four gold stars after each run, and it suddenly strikes you as ridiculous, a cheesy strategy to trick yourself into following through on a commitment. You know that it's important to stick to your goals, but there's something so annoying and fake about all that motivational philosophy. There's nothing at all inspiring about getting up in the morning. It sucks. Whose dumb idea was it to promise to exercise anyway? One day off won't matter that much. Besides, it feels a lot colder today. You close your eyes and feel the welcome lull of sleep coming over you again.

A few minutes later the alarm sounds again, and you hit the snooze once more. You're not feeling up for the exercise, and your knee was bothering you again yesterday, so it's probably better that you not push it too hard. You'd have to ice it down, and that extra time would make you late for work. Besides, you're definitely going to start back up tomorrow, which will give your knee a solid rest. You fall asleep again.

The alarm rings, but at this point it's too late to jog anyway. You hit snooze and drift off again.

In all of modern history, no single invention has so perfectly captured the perverse power of the mind to defeat its own best intentions as the snooze button. Situated precisely between your dreams and your waking life, the snooze button allows you to delay the inevitable with a minimum of true effort. When you hit the snooze button, you surrender power. Every grand resolution, every promise you've ever made to yourself, every good intention can be instantly wiped away with a simple press of a button. The snooze button is the perfect symbol of human resistance, and the emblem of anyone who feels stuck. Stuck in a dead-end job, stuck in a holding pattern, stuck in a stale relationship, stuck with a flabby body, stuck with a bunch of cool ideas that you never find the time to execute—just plain stuck.

When you're stuck, the snooze button is your best friend and your worst enemy. It allows you to stay in the comfortable confines of your hamster wheel. It allows you to effortlessly delay the real work of changing your life. No need to ask why we invented it—we already have a snooze button preinstalled inside us. It's always there if we want to use it. And use it we do. We come up with every imaginable excuse to delay, to avoid, and to stay stuck right where we are.

Take Alison for instance. She called into my show asking for advice about pursuing her dream to become a professional actress.

"How old are you, Alison?"

"Thirty-four."

"How long have you wanted to act?"

"My entire life. I've always wanted to be an actress. I dream about it," Alison says.

"When's the last time you acted?"

"I've never acted."

"What do you mean—never never?" I ask.

"Never."

"Why not?"

"I'm fat. I'm short. I'm scared."

"What are you scared of?"

"Being told I can't act," she says.

"What do you mean by that?"

"I'm worried if I tried, I'll be told I can't do it."

I can't make this stuff up. It's easy to judge Alison, but you do the exact same thing. For any part of your life that persistently makes you feel unhappy, you've created a million equally absurd reasons not to fix it.

Alison is trapped between her dream of being an actress and the paralysis she imposes by convincing herself to do nothing. You do the same thing every time you whine about problems but do nothing to fix them. You make excuse after excuse. "I don't have time." "I can't." "I might fail."

In her thirty-plus years, Alison has never tried out for a school play, taken an acting class, tried improv, or even signed up for Toastmasters. She tortures herself with this "dream," but presses snooze on every effort to change her life for the better. Her excuses are irrelevant. There are plenty of short, fat actresses in the twenty-first century, and they all have some level of fear to push through.

The irony of the situation is that Alison—by pressing snooze time after time—has made her worst nightmare a reality. She can't act, because she has told herself that she can't. By caving in to her inner resistance, she has already sealed the verdict on her acting career without even stepping outside her brain.

Behold the malevolent power of your inner snooze button to convert dreams into nightmares. She claims that fear prevents her from taking a step forward, but the truth is that showing up for a casting call in hot pink body paint might be less painful than the slow torture of living with a dream denied. So what's stopping Alison from taking a step forward?

Her brain. Over the years, Alison has avoided taking on any kind of challenge so many times that her brain is now primed to steer her clear of taking action. Her brain has grown to expect avoidance and to plan around it. All those calls for a change that surfaced in Alison whenever she felt inspired to become an actress should have tipped her into a commitment to take action. Instead she did nothing, and she's become stuck.

There have been thousands of moments in Alison's life when she thought about taking action: reciting lines in front of the mirror,

Googling "casting agent Kansas City," even watching contestants on reality shows amaze the world and wishing desperately that she could have a similar moment. Yet when the signal to take action sounds, Alison does nothing. She chooses to go nowhere.

Dreams and ambitions arise inside you as a signal, telling you that the powerful you is needed, right here, right now! The choice is always in front of you: Turn on the powerful you and move forward, or give in to resistance and go nowhere. If you take action, you can begin to build momentum and roll your life in small but new directions toward something you want, such as a better body, a better marriage, or something that might make you feel happier about where your life is going.

However, you don't take action, do you? You find different ways to let that dream fizzle. You give in to resistance, find some excuse, chicken out, and stay stuck. Every time you do that, you postpone your dreams. You rob yourself of happiness. You fall short of your true potential.

If you're tired of making the same promises to yourself and never keeping them, of making the same secret wishes over and over and never achieving them, of relying on "willpower" only to find that it isn't enough, then stick with me and keep reading.

You *can* have what you want, and I will teach you how. We will work together to figure out what you truly want, and build the momentum and stamina required to reach your true potential. You'll learn exactly what's behind the resistance you feel. I will show you metacognition tricks to outsmart your brain's self-defeating instincts. You will learn to recognize the signals for action and wake up and take control. Following my five-step method, you will locate the power switch inside you and learn how to turn it on.

You've hit the snooze button on your life for the last time.

What Feeling Stuck Is and What It Isn't

There's a name for that feeling just below the surface, when you know you want more from life but you don't know how to get it. When you constantly say things are fine while knowing that you really want something more. It's called *stuck*. Feeling stuck builds slowly from the inside like corrosion on a metal pipe. It's easy to miss because it starts with a vague feeling that something's a little off. There's no big, obvious problem to solve. On the surface, everything seems fine. But something is missing from your life and you can't quite put your finger on what it is, though some words come close—fulfillment, happiness, purpose, empowerment.

Instead of taking action, you placate your ambitions with excuses and rationalizations. You can't change your career. You don't have time to exercise. You can't find love. You can't start over.

But no matter how plausible these explanations sound on the surface, they are just rationalizations that let you avoid making a deeper commitment to achieving true satisfaction and happiness. These excuses keep you from heading in the right direction, taking control of your destiny, and becoming the person you want to be.

Of course, realizing your dreams is not going to be easy. It will require work and commitment from you. But you already know far too well the price of ignoring your dreams—that stuck feeling grows stronger inside you, it starts to undermine all aspects of your life, and if you don't confront the feeling and decide to make a true change, it will actually start to define you.

Feeling stuck is different from a crisis. When you face a crisis, your life crashes down all around you. A crisis comes the moment when you find the e-mail from your husband's secret lover, or your boss tells you that you're fired, or the doctor says, "I'm sorry, it's malignant." That's a crisis—and what you feel is not stuck. You feel panic. When a crisis hits all you care about is surviving. When people feel stuck, they paralyze themselves with worries about rocking the boat. When they're in crisis, the boat has just been hit by a cannonball.

The key difference between being stuck and being in crisis is your relationship to change. When you're in crisis, your life will change whether you like it or not. Your major task is how you manage the change. But when you're stuck, the major task is deciding if you're going to change at all. The challenge is finding the ability, in the face of an overwhelming amount of resistance, to create a small change in your life and build on it.

The only way to get unstuck is to force yourself to change and grow in meaningful ways. When you were younger you had all kinds of experiences to look forward to as an adult: college, moving out on your own, making your own money, blasting music, drinking, travel, dating, getting a "real" job. You were excited about what the future might hold. The last time most of us felt that type of optimism was on the eve of college graduation, anticipating what adult life would be like. "I'll get out in the real world and get a job where I can travel and manage people," you said to yourself. What a joke. The allure of travel wears off after a week on the road and managing people is a pain in the butt. You soon learn that a large part of adult life is spent standing in lines, waiting on hold, sitting in traffic, sending things to the printer, laying out PowerPoint presentations, and wasting your time in meetings. Your life quickly goes from waiting for something amazing to happen to assuming nothing will.

Marriages suffer from this same cycle. You start dating someone with wonder and anticipation, drunk on love. You romanticize everything about your partner, and even mundane activities like going to the grocery store together can seem like a fantastic date. But then you fall into a routine, and years later, you've become roommates, circling the same safe topics while packing lunches, the monotony broken only by occasional date nights.

Deep down, you know why these parts of your life have gone stale. It's because nothing new is happening. You may say you fear change, but the lack of change in your life is why you feel so blah. Monotony will drive any human relationship or endeavor into a ditch. That inner snooze button that lulls you into staying put is slowly killing you. At this point, you have no other choice. No one is coming to do this for you. You need to push yourself and move forward.

If you want more out of life, you must grow. Think about that for a minute because it makes sense. Every part of your body grows for your entire life: your hair, nails, and skin are constantly growing, and your cells regenerate every seven years. Your life needs to grow, too. If your life stops growing in new directions, you will start to feel a longing for more. As soon as you admit to yourself that you are no longer moving in the right direction or growing in ways that challenge and fulfill you, then you have the opportunity to change.

Circling, Spinning, and Thinking Leads You Nowhere

Deep down you probably have a pretty good sense of what you'd like to change. You most likely consider it quite often. Not in a fixated, obsessed kind of way, but as a droopy resignation that crosses your mind during the quiet moments when you're alone, drifting through the supermarket or riding home from work.

Colleen daydreams regularly about what she'd like to change in her life. She wants to meet someone great and get married. She's dressing in her one-bedroom apartment, putting on a wrap dress, mary jane heels, and her favorite Coach handbag. She stops and stares in the mirror by the door to check herself out before heading off to work.

Perhaps today is the day. She wants nothing more than to find the right person, fall in love, and start a family. Particularly that last part—at forty-two, she's already certain she'll have trouble getting pregnant. She wraps the scarf around her neck the way she learned at the boutique in Paris where she bought it last year. That European adventure was another all-girls trip. At this point, she'll be the last from her circle of friends to get married. One of them is already divorced. "Thank God," Colleen thought when she heard the news. Of course she felt "bad" for Julie, but at least now she'll have a dinner partner again.

She colors her lips with a cocoa-toned lipstick and wonders for a moment if she should be wearing something brighter. Forty-two. Single and successful. *Why is this happening to me? Why can't I meet anyone?* She walks out the front door down four flights of stairs. She picks up her newspaper lying next to the stroller in the lobby and feels a small pang in her heart. *When will it be my turn?*

Like Colleen, you've probably circled around the changes you want to make to your life the way a dog circles a tree full of squirrels: lose eighty pounds, start a business, stop smoking, build a house, meet someone, bank a million, find your passion. There's no way you're possibly going to make those changes happen any more than that dog will actually climb that tree, and you can list a hundred different reasons why, but you keep looking up and checking to see if those squirrels are still there.

Sometimes as you circle that tree, you might realize that you're stuck in a loop. You keep making the same resolutions over and over. Richard Wiseman, a psychologist at Britain's University of

Hertfordshire, found in a recent study that 88 percent of people fail to keep their resolutions. That's not news to anyone who's made one. You are fired up to train for a marathon on January 1, but by the fifth morning even those gold stars on your calendar in the closet can't lure you from your warm bed.

You want to change, but you never seem to be able to follow through, or you don't ever take the steps to really make it happen. Or like Colleen, you don't have a clue what to do differently. You've probably tried several times to make a small change but have given up after a few strikeouts, or gotten sidetracked, or faced too much scorn and resistance from others. Or maybe you are just too intimidated by the prospect, because you know your own limits too well, so you don't even bother. No one feels likes doing the work to change. But powerful people do it anyway. That's the difference between someone who is stuck and someone who makes things happen in life. The powerful you figures out how to stop circling the tree and take real action.

Brian spends fifteen hours in traffic every week to get to work. This evening the interstate is at a standstill. "Must be an accident," he thinks. He flips through the channels on the radio looking for a traffic report. His mind drifts to the evening ahead. Jennifer will be home by now with the boys. By the time Brian gets home, they'll be plugged into their laptops and doing homework in their rooms, and he'll be eating dinner alone in the kitchen while Jennifer does the dishes. They'll talk, but not really about anything. He wonders momentarily if they'll have sex tonight; it's been months.

He thinks back to college, remembering when he had the freedom to jump into a crappy old car and visit a friend five hundred miles away, or go to parties and meet new and exciting people who would challenge his perspective. He remembers when he landed a real job, and tasted his first real financial success. He wonders, as he has on so many drives home, how he ended up here trapped in a job he hates just so he can pay his bills.

Then he starts to think about Molly, as he does whenever he starts to get depressed. She started working at the company four months ago, and their connection was immediate. It was clearly more than professional for both of them, though they played it cool. In the past several weeks she's gone from a simple distraction to someone whom he actually can't stop thinking about. They can talk about things that he can't discuss with Jennifer. They e-mail all weekend long and check in on text. He has crossed emotional boundaries, but no physical ones—which doesn't stop him from fantasizing endlessly about having sex with her. Some days he prays for a conference or a business trip where he has a built-in excuse to get drunk and make a "mistake."

His cell phone beeps. A new text is in. "Hey, honey, boys have eaten. What's ur eta?" Brian's heart sinks. "I can't do that to Jennifer. I have to stop this before it goes too far." He thinks about sending Molly a text—"I can't do this." But he doesn't want to end this wonderful distraction and is annoyed at the prospect that he should. It's the first time in a decade he has looked forward to work and Jennifer is always "tired." He wonders for a minute how he ever ended up in the mortgage industry. He scans the last twenty years, looking for the wrong turn. He keeps coming back to the decision to get out of retail sales and go into management. Back then, Brian had hated what sales required: the cold-calling, haggling with inspectors over valuation, scanning the obituaries and pitching widows on cashing out of their homes and downsizing. He wanted to change careers and start a business, but the boys were little and Jennifer wanted to stay home, so he didn't push it. He took the most comfortable route: a lateral move into corporate. Now he feels like he is stuck on this track forever. He worries about paying the mortgage, car payments, insurance, and college tuition. A midlevel manager in a dying industry is not where Brian expected to be at forty-four.

The feeling that you are trapped by the life you have created is terrifying and infuriating. Deep down, you know you want something more, but maybe you don't know what it is or you simply don't have a clue how to get it.

Brian is annoyed with how life has turned out. Frankly, it's turned him into a jerk. He complains to himself that life isn't fair, that the company is the problem. He blames Jennifer's lack of intimacy for his fantasies about Molly. With Brian, there's plenty of blame to pass around, as long as it doesn't land on him. When you think like Brian, nothing is your fault. It's the perfect way to keep from facing your own problems and your need to change. When you can't get what you want out of life, it's easy to start acting like a jerk. Your inability to change your life and be more fulfilled frustrates the heck out of you, which clouds your mind.

If Brian were being powerful, he'd be doing what he doesn't feel like doing. He'd end the dangerous flirtation with Molly, he'd get into counseling with Jennifer, and he'd write a business plan and launch something on the side instead of surfing the Web and scouring the past for mistakes. It's obvious what he should do, right? And it's clear that he is miserable. So it begs the question: Why doesn't he do it? The same reason you don't: *He doesn't feel like it.*

There are days that Colleen feels so scared that she'll always be alone that she can barely get out of bed and face the day. She sees couples everywhere she goes and has recently started to give up on having a family of her own. The guys she meets online don't last beyond the first meeting over coffee and a dinner date. She can't figure out why she can't meet anyone, when all her friends have had such luck. She's got a good body, comes from a great family, and has a solid career—but she's alone. Will she ever have kids? Will she ever find love? She's so afraid of disappointment that she can't be herself when she meets someone new. She comes on either too strong or too eager. She's so afraid of not being liked that she can't act normal. Instead of trying to relax and just get out more, Colleen is cooling on the idea of dating altogether. If Brian's resistance is turning him into a jerk, then Colleen's has made her a chicken. And just as Brian's anger is keeping him from thinking clearly, Colleen's fear is overriding her good judgment.

If Colleen were being powerful, she would explore ways to get what she wants more than anything—a child. She would learn about adoption, being a foster parent, or single parenting by choice. She would end the ban on divorced men with children and see what dating one feels like. Friends have made these suggestions dozens of times. She's clearly unhappy and not having success with her approach, so why is she pulling back instead of pushing ahead and exploring options? For the same reasons you don't force yourself to push ahead and explore ways to change your life. *She's afraid.*

Whether it is fear or frustration or both, the thought of trying to change your life can feel like trying to turn around an eighteen-wheeler in a packed parking lot. It's your feelings about it all that keep you stuck. If it doesn't "feel like" a good idea, you don't do it. That's the problem!

Action: The Enemy of Stuck

It's obvious, right? Take action. But if it is so simple, why don't you take the steps needed to make a change? Is modern life somehow more difficult? Or is it your fault because you lack the strength, stamina, or drive to really be successful? Is it just a natural part of growing up and coming to terms with your limitations?

It's easy to blame the problem on circumstances such as time, money, or all the little details that get in the way and undercut your energy. There's no doubt that modern life has gotten more complicated. You deal with decisions and situations every day that your grandparents never had to face. The uncertainty of life in the twenty-first century has a big impact on your personal ability and capacity to change. The effort needed to switch cell-phone carriers— never mind your job—is enough to send you spinning. And in the midst of all the confusion, it can seem as if some of the most important stuff starts to get mixed up with all the everyday stuff, until you feel as if the direction of your day hinges on trivial details such as finding a sock from the laundry that's missing its mate, or forgetting to return a phone call, or the mood of your spouse at dinner. You have given up on ever making a serious change in your own life, just so you can get through the day.

But the real reason you get stuck has nothing to do with technology or chores, and everything to do with you and who's in charge of your head. You listen to how you feel. You stop yourself when you feel afraid or annoyed, instead of doing the hard work to transform your desires into something solid and real by taking action.

Most people are like you, overworked and trampled by the demands of their life. But you don't have to be part of that 88 percent crowd that hits the snooze, breaks their resolutions, and delays their dreams. You can get what you want, and you can be happy. You can be a filmmaker and a mom. You can have a trim tummy and a full-time job. You can find love and have a child. You can learn a new language and live overseas. You can have a hot marriage and start a new business.

And perhaps most important, you can get what you want without blowing up your life. You simply must adopt a powerful mindset and push yourself to take action when you don't feel like it. To be powerful, you must make it happen while you worry that you can't. You must push yourself to do the things you don't want to do, so you can become the person you were meant to be. If Alison ignores how she feels, she can be an actor. Colleen can have a child if she pushes past her fears. Brian can work with Jennifer to improve their marriage and launch a side business if he'd just stop complaining and start taking action. You can have what you want, too. There's nothing stopping you from achieving your goals but you and your dumb-ass excuses. Perhaps you've heard that so many times it sounds like a fairy tale. It is a fact. **You can stay where you are, or you can change your life. Of course it takes effort, but it's not as hard as you believe, and I'm going to prove it to you.**

The Problem Is You

What's the biggest obstacle between you and the life you want? I'm sure money, time, experience, and circumstances come to mind. You're wrong. The biggest obstacle you face is you. You're in your own way.

You've adopted a rigid mind-set that is preventing you from changing. A mind-set is like a pair of sunglasses that filters all your thoughts and feelings. If you put on a pair of sunglasses with amber-colored lenses, for example, it colors everything you see with a tint of brownish yellow. Rose-colored lenses make the world appear pink. You get the idea. Sunglasses change what you see.

A mind-set changes what you think and feel. Depending on your mind-set, your ideas either take flight or fizzle into nothing. If you looked at the world through a more powerful mind-set, you could take on and accomplish anything.

But right now, you've got a negative mind-set about change in place. It's become so instinctual, you probably don't even realize what you're doing. Whenever you start thinking about changing something in your life or trying something new, you shade the idea with so much negativity, you kill it altogether. We've all heard the term *victim mentality* used to describe someone who always sees himself or herself as a victim. It's easy to see in others but tough to spot in ourselves. Luckily, Lauren Zander, who teaches The Handel Method™ for life change at MIT and Stanford business schools, boils it down to two mind-sets: the chicken and the jerk. I love these two labels because they make it super easy to spot which one you use to kill your dreams. If you ever catch yourself acting like a chicken or a jerk, wake the hell up—you are not being powerful! Let me show you how this works.

Alison wants to be an actress. But when she is sitting at her desk and the thought rises in her head *I should just Google "auditions Kansas City,"* instead of being powerful and acting on the idea—she becomes a chicken. She starts thinking about stage fright and rejections, and convinces herself *she's not ready* and puts off action, yet again. You do the same thing. When fear starts to creep in and you find yourself waging a campaign to delay action—WAKE UP!—you are being a chicken and pecking your dreams to death with "What Ifs." You must turn on that power inside and take action regardless of how you feel.

Brian wants to get out of the mortgage business. But when he sees an interesting franchise advertised in the back of a magazine instead of calling the 800 number for more information—the jerk steps in. He feels annoyed about the money it would require and how much time he's wasted in the mortgage industry, and then the dream becomes a "dumb idea" and disappears. You do the same thing. When thinking about change just makes you more frustrated and annoyed about the situation you are currently in—WAKE UP!—you

Identify Your Negative Mind-set	CHICKEN	JERK
What you say to yourself	I can't. I'm not ready. I'm scared. What if I fail? I don't know how. I might make a fool of myself. People will laugh. I'm not good enough. What if . . .	I don't want to. Why me? I don't feel like it. It doesn't matter anyway. It's his fault; he should have to fix this. What difference is it going to make? If only I had . . . I should have . . .
What you feel inside	Fear, nerves, anxiety, worry, concern, paralysis, overwhelmed, unworthiness	Anger, frustration, blame, smarminess, sarcasm, resignation, stubbornness, annoyance, impatience
What you should expect	It will feel terrifying and radical to force yourself to act because of the wall of fear the chicken has built up in your brain. But once you make a small move forward and see that you didn't die, nothing bad happened, and it wasn't as painful as you told yourself it would be . . . the fear will slowly start to dissolve. With every push forward, the chicken in your mind will get quieter and quieter until you no longer hear clucking at all.	The powerful you must go head to head with the jerk in your brain. You will never feel like it. You will argue against taking action. You will call yourself and the idea itself "stupid." You will want to give up and you will try every way possible to bully yourself into stopping. The powerful you must just ignore this bullying and push ahead. Expect your brain to wage a campaign against moving forward until you start racking up a couple of small wins. Only with a few hard-fought wins will the jerk in your brain actually start to shut up.
Your mantra	"Shut up. I'm doing it anyway."	"Shut up. I'm doing it anyway."

are being a jerk and stomping out all motivation to move forward and explore. You must turn on that power inside and take action even though you don't feel like it!

It may sound a little simplistic or cheesy to you. But getting what you want in life really does boil down to these little moments when either your negative mind-set takes control or the powerful you steps in and pushes forward.

You don't have what you want because your thoughts and feelings hold you back. Your resistance to change, whether it manifests as fear or anger or stubbornness, keeps you on the safe, familiar path. Allowing a chicken or a jerk to run your life never ends well.

So what do you do when the chicken or the jerk is killing your motivation to act? The fix is not about making bold five-year plans, or locking yourself into death-march marathon efforts. It's about becoming more powerful in small ways on a daily basis. By taking action (when you don't feel like it), you can start to steer your life in new directions. You see, action is its own reward. Every new action you make, and every positive step you take toward change, will provide you with the inspiration and energy to take the next step. Every positive action creates momentum to supply the next action. When you start building momentum, you're creating a perpetual motion machine that will give you enough energy to face the next challenge. Your challenge is simply to stop hitting the snooze and start. Not tomorrow. Not next week. Not next year. Start taking action now.

It sounds simple, but don't kid yourself. It will take work and you'll need to build stamina to rebuild that bridge between idea and action. You need to follow a recipe that helps you defeat the chicken and jerk mind-sets that you consider normal.

Stick with this book, and you'll start seeing the world in a whole new way. You'll start to see the mental traps you set for yourself throughout your day. You'll understand how the world you live in pushes your psychological snooze buttons. One by one, we'll dismantle them together. And you will realize the only way to get what you want is to stop saying you're fine and learn how to be powerful, especially when you don't feel like it.

Modern Life Makes You Feel Stuck

A feeling of control is the foundation of human happiness. When you feel like there are too many things outside your control, you start feeling powerless and unhappy. When you feel like your own actions can't make a true difference in the direction of your life, you start giving up. And that's the precise moment that you become stuck.

There's something about life today that makes it easy to get stuck. The outside world operates on your inner well-being. Between the increasingly frantic pace of daily life, financial problems, and an endless stream of distractions, it's no wonder that you feel like you can't really be your best. You're simply spending less time focusing on yourself. When you're surrounded by change, and you're constantly adapting to new conditions, it lowers your own desire and ability to change.

The world has totally changed beneath your feet and it has an enormous impact on how you feel. The economy has been undergoing seismic changes since the start of the 1980s. Hundreds of thousands of jobs have moved overseas, and the American economy has moved away from the stability of heavy manufacturing industries into a more volatile, service-driven system. The Web has exploded the amount of information you process every day, and created the need to adapt to a constant series of new gadgets and ideas. The ultimate effect of all this change on society is still unknown. The only thing that's not in dispute is the fact that there is a negative effect on your brain. New problems and new decisions arrive at your doorstep each week. Whether it's deciding how much television or Internet your kids can watch, or the shadow of unemployment hanging over your house, or just trying to eat healthfully, you feel a constant sense that you're just barely keeping up. The modern world teaches you that there are too many things out of your control.

As if all these external factors weren't enough, your own mind begins working against you, too. As the world inserts all sorts of uncertainties into your life, your mind supplements them by installing its own doubts. When you feel stuck, you become acutely aware of what's missing in your life. Your mind tries to figure out what's wrong, and focuses on the past, highlighting and even inventing a series of missteps. Every caller to my radio show raises them: Emily was "married too young," Michael has "bills to pay," Stephanie and her husband, Aaron, "grew apart," Kathy "didn't know anything else was possible," and Sarah put her dreams "on hold when the kids where born." You start to see the decisions in your life not as a series of small victories, but as a series of sacrifices that you've made, composed of a routine that you must endure, the details of which are beyond your control.

Of course, on the path to adulthood, you are forced to make big decisions that impact the direction of your life. The schools you attend, the jobs you accept, the monthly nut you need to cover, the friends you keep, maybe marriage and children—these decisions stick with you for a long time. But when you're in a negative frame of mind, and you feel stuck, you start to rewrite history. As you look backward on each decision, and the path you took, you become more aware of the things you left behind. You twist these decisions that once were powerful symbols of your achievements, and start viewing them as sacrifices. Instead of seeing what a new job brought to your life, you begin to think about all the other jobs it cut you off from. Instead of seeing your marriage as a step toward building a truly adult relationship, you frame it as a burden that keeps you from growing individually.

And to complete the knot, there doesn't seem to be any time to fix the problem. The demands of life can seem all-consuming. Sometimes it feels as if there's no time to move outside the daily routine and do something different. After a long week, you look back and it can feel as if you had no spare time to do something interesting just for yourself. What could you possibly have done to really make a meaningful change in your own life, when you can't even find the time to get a wax?

These internal and external forces reinforce and maintain a feeling of being stuck. The uncertainty caused by the economic climate, combined with the trap of daily routine, and the sense of sacrifice from unrealized dreams all create a spellbinding illusion that you lack control. If you hear yourself ever saying "It is what it is," that's not the powerful you talking.

Control cuts to the heart of our lives. A lack of control inspires all sorts of negative philosophical questions. Without control, you start to question your place in life, where you are headed, and what is the point of it all. Were my expectations too high? Is my life really supposed to be this unfulfilling? Is there something wrong with me?

You start to feel hopeless and too afraid to try anything new. You get mad and start acting like a jerk. You find yourself jealous of people who have more than you. You adopt a victim mentality and judge the world critically in order to make yourself feel better. Obviously, these mind-sets keep you stuck.

But as you'll learn, despite the fact that you cast the problem in such a dramatic light, it's really not hard to fix. You'll find that if you can simply regain a very small amount of control over your life—by being more powerful and creating the time to do the things that truly inspire you and bring passion into your life—you will feel very different.

In fact, if you can reclaim control over 5 percent of your life, and spend that time doing something productive, energy-inspiring, and action-oriented, you will quickly restore order and balance to your life. You will find all the routine, uncertainty, and difficulty significantly more tolerable. You will discover that this small 5 percent acts like an anchor to reorient your whole perspective. Once you've achieved that small foothold, many things fall back into place.

But brace yourself, that first 5 percent is the hardest part.

Action Is the Key to Everything

Action is the key to becoming more powerful. An action is a thought brought to life. Something as simple as getting up from your chair and stepping outside began with a thought. "I'm feeling cooped up," you think, and suddenly you're outside in the fresh air. You thought about it, and somehow it happened. That's a kind of magic, and too often we don't really appreciate just how special taking action really can be. The sheer satisfaction from turning a wish—"I wish my room was clean"—into reality can be very fulfilling.

Compare it to other situations where you are passive. You're in a train and watching the scenery pass by. You're on your couch and watching a television chase scene through the streets of Rome. You're at work and listening to your boss summarize last year's performance. You recognize someone at a party, but don't dare say hello.

All of these situations put a buffer between what you're thinking and what you can actually do about it. You're just a spectator. When you take action, your thoughts animate your body with purpose, and your body changes some small part of the world.

Discover a *More Powerful You*

TO combat your mind-set, adopt the five-second rule. Move from idea to execution in five seconds. Pretend that if you don't, the idea will start to melt. The longer you wait, the more likely you'll have only a puddle left to work with. If you think that's not enough time, guess again. Five seconds is a lifetime for your brain and plenty of time for your thoughts and feelings to step in and kill the idea. Your brain can read the expression on someone's face in less than thirty-three milli-seconds, and your first instincts are often more correct than your second-guesses. Your brain can surely make up its mind quicker than you allow. So try it. What's something you've been putting off? Take one small action now. The longer your idea sits there, the less likely you'll take action.

Action unites body and mind. Every action starts with an inner, mental impulse and finishes with a physical gesture that rubs you up against the fabric of the world. Action is your own personal bridge from inside to outside.

The feeling of control is tightly linked to action. When you can take action and see positive results in the world, you feel powerful. But when you feel that your actions don't make any difference in the world, or that it's hardly even worth taking an action, you feel hopeless and unhappy.

Something feels broken inside when you're stuck. Your mind is still working fine, because you can perfectly imagine the way your life should be going. Your thoughts give a very clear picture of the way things are supposed to be. You keep looking for ways to make a change. But something is preventing your deepest desires from translating into a concrete action. The connection is broken and it's probably because the jerk or the chicken is in charge of your decisions.

Every experience in every moment of your life contains two primary elements: one is the outside world, the setting and circumstances that frame the moment. The other is the set of feelings, thoughts, and attitudes within you that both drive and respond to the moment. When you feel as though you lack control over your life, it's because you feel that both parts are preventing you from taking meaningful action. You're locked up, as if both your inner and outer worlds are ganging up to keep you from moving forward. You must start by taking back control of your head if you want to gain control over your life.

Don't package your dreams as a huge accomplishment or you'll feel chicken and never start. Rather, coax yourself into action by focusing on the steps in the organic process or on merely getting started. First of all, you probably feel overwhelmed and intimidated by the size and scale of change that would be needed to make a true difference in your life. Alison, for example, has a clear idea of what she wants (to be a "real" actor), and she's packaged that idea as the result. So when she thinks about the change she wants to make in her life, instead of viewing it as an organic process, she sees herself at the premiere of her first movie talking to the paparazzi.

Of course, when you picture it like that, the change feels so enormous that only a mammoth or explosive effort could rocket you there. It feels completely out of the question that you'll just drop a grenade into your life, move to L.A., conquer a lifetime of stage fright, and make a go of it as an actor. You've got commitments and responsibilities, bills to pay, and family members who rely on your support. You also know that real, lasting change in your life requires hard work, and perhaps a level of discipline and willpower that you simply don't possess. And perhaps most frustrating, you just can't seem to summon the energy to really do something about it. There are too many obligations and distractions that keep you from really spending the time on it. You start to feel a little chicken about the whole idea, so you start acting like one and don't even try.

Don't try to find the right way to get started or you'll soon start to feel frustrated and become a jerk about it. Rather, push yourself to just start without it being perfect and move forward and improve from there. You also have to deal with all of the uncertainty that surrounds your goal. You have a hard time imagining exactly how you're going to achieve it. The world today is so complex and unforgiving. There's no instruction manual for life, and you probably don't have a network of knowledgeable people to help you, or the experience required to break into something completely new. Without knowing how to do something, it feels impossible to dive in and start doing it. You're bound to make costly mistakes, end up with egg on your face, and perhaps ruin your chances right at the start. That just makes you even angrier. Brian already can't stand how his career has turned out and he's afraid to make another bad career move. He punishes himself every time he sees the balance in his checking account. He feels like throttling the mortgage brokers in the office when they ring the bell, the sign of another deal closed and commission dollars rolling into their bank accounts, not his.

It's important to realize that all these negative feelings are only half right. Yes, you want to kick yourself for some dumb decisions you've made. And it's true that the change you want to make is probably big, and the world doesn't let people cut to the front of the line on a smile. It takes real work to make things happen.

But amid all the fear and anger, you have forgotten about the most powerful ally in the world—yourself. Your inner world is completely under your control. Your emotions may feel overwhelming, the world may be pushing your buttons constantly, and those chicken and jerk feelings may undermine you at every turn, but you can regain control. You can start thinking bigger. Bigger than this moment. Bigger than this obstacle. Bigger than your fears and your frustrations. That's the powerful you—it's always bigger than the fears you feel. If the powerful you is in charge, you'll push ahead and start taking the small series of steps that add up to change. That's how you get what you want in life. And you will start to see the results of your effort almost immediately.

Without consciously and actively nurturing the kind of approach that lets you see something bigger for yourself and rebuild the bridge between idea and action, you will continue to fall into the same traps you've already sprung on yourself. You will continue to allow your feelings and thoughts to interrupt the path from dream to reality, and sap the energy that drives real change.

You Are Not Fine

The first and most important step is to stop saying you are fine. You are not fine. You need to quit pretending that you are, and state for the record what's bothering you. There is a lot more in store for you than what you've got going on right now, and the first step to getting it is to stop pretending that everything is okay.

With that simple confession, you will be in great company, and on your way. A while back, I listened to the late Reverend Peter Gomes, a renowned theologian from Harvard University. He's a classic Boston Brahmin of the twenty-first century, by way of Cape Verde, and a spiritual legend. If I'd been picking someone on this planet immune from feeling stuck in his life, I'd have put money on Peter Gomes.

But on that day, as I listened to one of his sermons, he said, "I have grown tired of where I am. I am tired of my small-mindedness. I am tired of my excuses. I am tired of who I am. I am tired of pretending that I have it all figured out. I want to become something more than who I am today. Who I am today is not who I am meant to become. My quest is the same as yours. The question we all face is: What about yourself are you willing to shed to become who you were meant to be?"

When he said that, all the brainiacs and overachievers filling Harvard's church that day collectively exhaled. When Gomes admitted that he felt stuck, it allowed everyone to momentarily drop the facade. We're all frustrated by some aspect of our lives. We want to be something bigger than we are. It's built into our DNA. As long as you are breathing, you will be looking for something more. What you decide to do with that feeling determines everything about your life.

A woman called my radio show recently, and she wanted help losing sixty pounds. When I pressed her, she admitted that the number was closer to one hundred pounds. When I pressed her further, she admitted that it's been an issue for years and then revealed her inner reason for why she hadn't felt motivated. Until now. "Well, you know. It's not that big of a deal. That's why I haven't done anything. It's not like I have three hundred pounds to lose." She had convinced herself that it wasn't that bad. But it was bad. She beat herself up about her weight every day. She hated looking in the mirror. Hated shopping for clothes and felt horrible about her declining health. It was bad.

Everyone does this. We are all stuck in some area of our life, pretending it's *not that bad* so we can justify doing nothing. You do it, too. You persuade yourself that things are not *that bad* because you don't want to have to change. You also minimize the situation when you don't know how to change something. **Ironically, the more trapped you feel by your life, the more you'll convince yourself it's okay.**

When you finally cut the baloney and admit it, you'll be faced with the sobering reality of how much work is in front of you. That's why the caller who was one hundred pounds overweight couldn't tell the truth that a hundred pounds was a lot. That amount actually scared her. She couldn't bring herself to say that she was shocked that it had climbed that high and felt terribly discouraged. It was so much easier to pretend that she's not "that" fat and do nothing. This is a classic move. When you are afraid, it's easier to convince yourself to do nothing than to deal with the thought of failing again.

We don't want to tell the truth because lying to ourselves and justifying inaction is the only way we can avoid having to face the fear of taking a risk. As soon as you tell the truth, you blow up your coping mechanisms. If Brian were to stop being a jerk about his life and face the truth, he would feel like a failure. By downplaying it all with an air of anger, Brian avoids feeling what's just beneath the tough surface: profound sadness that his life isn't turning out as he'd hoped.

You downplay your disappointment in life. Everyone does. No one wants to tell the truth about what he really wants and how he really feels about his life. Especially when you see friends with cooler lives than you on Facebook, hear about people who somehow turned it all around, or watch perfect strangers get made over on reality television. The pressure to make sure that you are keeping up is everywhere. But keeping up with appearances won't help you take action. It's not powerful. You cannot get what you want if you refuse to face the truth. You are struggling. You long for more. We all do. That tension between where you are now and what you want to become is what makes you human.

There really is a method to changing your life and taking control of your head. I'm not pretending it's rocket science, but it is too hard to go at it alone. You've already proven to yourself that you're susceptible to hitting snooze and getting stuck. You know that you've got the capacity to undermine your own goals. This time, try it my way.

CHAPTER TWO

Anti-Actions, Fake Limits, and Other Ways Your Brain Betrays You

There's a battle going on in your brain, and it's keeping you from getting what you want. To win any fight you have to know what you are up against and how to fight back. Your brain is a formidable opponent and it fights dirty. At crucial moments throughout your day, your brain is putting the brake on your desire for action and inserting thoughts and feelings in order to keep you from moving forward. Yes, you read that right. You don't have the life you want because your brain is keeping you from getting it. It pits your feelings against your dreams. It sets your worries against your ambitions. And it tees up your frustrations against your future. You are going to learn how to fight back and win. I will hand you an arsenal of tools to use to lift the brake in your brain and take charge of your life, but first you've got to understand how your mind traps you.

Your brain has made an art form out of doing nothing through "anti-actions." Anti-actions are the actions you take in the place of the ones you need to take. You can find examples of anti-actions everywhere in your life.

- You want a raise at work, but you convince yourself to put in the minimum amount of effort possible, telling yourself "no one cares about this thing anyway." Putting in a minimum amount of effort is an anti-action. If you were more powerful, you'd go beyond just phoning it in and put yourself in a position to argue for the raise.

- You want to get back in shape, but every day you take anti-actions that waste the time you could have spent on training at the gym. You hit the snooze, surf the Web, take a little longer at lunch, or run an errand that isn't really urgent. All these anti-actions create just enough of a squeeze on your time that you can convince yourself that you don't have the time to hit the gym tonight.

- You want to figure out what to do with your life now that the kids are off to school, but you convince yourself that you're not really qualified to do anything because you haven't worked in over a decade and you are "just a mom." Instead of looking for a job, getting advice from old colleagues, or attending a weekend seminar to help you create the next chapter of your life, you throw yourself into projects around the house like updating photo albums or rearranging the living room. There's a small rush of satisfaction from getting these projects done, but they undermine your true desires. These anti-actions dismiss the hundreds of hours of volunteer fund-raising work you've done for the school and the innate project management skills you possess due to managing three kids' sports, music, homework, and after-school schedules.

Your feelings and mind-set are driving these anti-actions and interrupting the natural course of energy from thought to action, and keep you spinning in circles without growing or changing.

Where are these feelings coming from? Why does your brain undercut itself? Recent research over the past decade has come a long way toward helping us understand what feelings really are and how they operate. Through all sorts of advances in different fields of psychology and visualization, researchers have drawn some solid conclusions about the nature of our feelings, which overturn some of our earlier notions about how the mind works.

We all know that our minds are divided into conscious and unconscious levels of thinking. Our traditional understanding of the unconscious mind, whether Freudian or Jungian, was a vast store-house of hidden thoughts and desires, kept out of reach of our every-day thoughts. There was always an air of someone hidden behind the curtains. But as modern technology allows us to uncover, isolate, and see the mind at work, we're starting to get a different picture of the unconscious mind as a complex, layered set of automatic pro-cesses, what Dr. Timothy Wilson of Harvard University calls the "automatic unconscious."

We're discovering that many of our feelings are just a kind of sophisticated shorthand for all sorts of complex calculations that are constantly occurring in the back of your brain. Your feelings are a way of taking tons of incoming data and delivering it to your con-scious mind as kind of fuzzy sentiment to steer your decisions. In other words, your unconscious mind may be a lot less of a wizard behind the curtain, and a lot more like a bunch of very fast proces-sors all working together, like the ones Wall Street traders use to make many decisions very quickly.

The problem we're discovering with our minds, however, is

that these unconscious automatic processors have some evolutionary shortcomings. They are impressively fast, and excellent tools for
most kinds of decision making that involve survival, but they're not
so good at some of the subtleties of higher-level thinking. As a result,
we are constantly making predictably irrational errors. For example,
our brains have a terrible bias for "now" over "later," because our
automatic unconscious believes that survival depends on immediate
satisfaction. We will gladly sacrifice true happiness later for a good
time now. Remember that list of things that resistance loves: surfing the Web, vegging out in front of the TV, sticking to routine,
not picking up the phone, hitting snooze, avoiding confrontation,
making excuses, rumination, and isolation. Every last one of those
feels like the right thing to do in the moment. That's why your brain
opts to do it.

**To grow, you have to do the stuff that feels hard right
now, not later.** There are scores of other examples, and we'll cover
the most important ones in this chapter. The point is that when
it comes to getting unstuck, you've got your work cut out for you.
That's because there are two basic forces at work in your brain. On
the one hand, you have an imagination that is devising new and
interesting ideas for your life. On the other hand, you've got an automatic unconscious that's weighing risk at every step of your life, and
it is trying to discreetly (i.e., without your consent) veto any ideas or
actions that might lead to what it considers a dangerous (by cave-
man standards) change.

It's a constant battle between your game-changer thoughts (*lose
weight, start a business, find love*) that want to upset the current order
of your life, and the protective thoughts (*I don't feel like it today,
what if I get hurt*) that want to preserve order by keeping things the
same. Your mind is always scouting all the incoming signs from the
outside world, and trying to make predictions about what might

happen next, all in order to maintain a high level of safety and a reduced level of risk. When it sees a threat of any kind, it finds a reason to retreat. It's the wet-blanket theory of motivation. If your mind can kill a great idea by dampening it with emotional turmoil, it will.

Alison sees a poster at Starbucks advertising local theater auditions for the summer production of *Rent*. She reads it and thinks about tearing off one of the tabs with a phone number to call for more information. Her mind immediately starts to predict what might happen next. She envisions a long line of people waiting to try out, forgetting her lines, and a large rash breaking out on her neck. Thank you, wet-blanket theory!

Resistance is about never living in the moment. You're always worried about the future and your predictions. It's a deliberate interruption of what you're feeling right now, and heightening the fear and anxiety levels due to what you think is coming up. You think about possible futures, and avoid them. As a result, you're failing to live in the moment and missing out on capitalizing on opportunities right in front of your face.

Colleen is so worried about being single for the rest of her life that she misses out on opportunities to build her confidence and meet men every day. As she walks to work, she usually has her face planted in her BlackBerry, texting with friends or checking dating sites, and in the process she cuts off any chance she might have of making a spontaneous connection with the people around her. The guy behind her at the ATM thinks she's really cute, but she's standing there with her arms crossed, staring at the wall worried about being late. Rather than living her day-to-day life with an air of openness to meeting people, she's become insular, preoccupied, and uptight.

Colleen needs to stop obsessing over her fear of being alone and start practicing forming connections with the strangers she meets every day, by making eye contact, smiling, and sending off an "open" and fun vibe. If you see someone whom you are attracted to, are you more likely to say hello if she is smiling or if she is scowling with her arms crossed? Even in the age of easy online dating, at some point you'll have to go offline and connect in person. You might as well start practicing now. I subscribe to the "you never know where this will lead" philosophy of change. Since you never know where things might lead, the only thing you need to do is put something into play. Too often we take ourselves out of the game of life by thinking there's a right time to go for it, or we so overengineer the way we plan to start, we never start at all.

You can go for it today. Here's how you start—you simply act as if you already have what you desire. Instead of hiding behind fear, Colleen must manufacture the air of happiness and confidence that she would have if she were already in a great relationship. No worry. No obsession. Alison would stare at that poster and tap the powerful side of her that already was an actress, and she'd rip that tab off with authority.

Faking your confidence is powerful. That kind of investment in yourself that's made when you take action (even though you are quaking inside) will boost your confidence and your attractiveness in ways that no cropped-just-right Match.com photo, spray tan, or teeth whitener ever could.

The trick to getting unstuck is giving the powerful you control of your actions so that the chicken, the jerk, and the wet-blanket predictions that your brain lays on you don't take control and screw you over. Alison and Colleen both have opportunities for improving their lives sitting right in front of them, and the only thing holding them back is their preoccupation with an awful, but completely fictional, future their brain just invented.

Discover a *More Powerful You*

THESE are the seven major areas of your life.
Consider each one for a moment, and then you will
answer the questions below to figure out whether
you act like a chicken or a jerk in each area.
Identifying it now will help you catch yourself in
the moment later.

> Family
> Love
> Spirituality
> Career/Purpose
> Friends/Community
> Body/Health
> Money

Here's how Colleen filled this out:

FAMILY   I'm being a chicken around my mother. I don't want to tell her that I'm thinking about doing this baby thing on my own. I'm afraid my parents won't support that decision. They are so traditional, and so Catholic. How are they going to feel about a sperm bank and how am I going to raise a baby on my own?

LOVE   I'm being a jerk with men. I'm mad no one has picked me. I don't trust them and I'm afraid to open up. I'm starting to talk myself into thinking that I don't want one. Sex life is sad. I miss sex. I'd really like to have someone fun to sleep with, at the least.

SPIRITUALITY This is good. I meditate. I go to yoga. Content.

CAREER/PURPOSE Career is good, but purpose in life scares me. I'm afraid that I'll never have a family of my own. I always thought I'd have a family by now! Never occurred to me that I wouldn't have kids. I don't want to miss my opportunity and I'm afraid if I don't do something drastic, I will miss my window to have a child of my own.

FRIENDS/COMMUNITY I have a very strong group of girlfriends from college. I just want a man! Sometimes I feel jealous of their marriages or children, but it fades quickly. I don't know what I'd do without the support of my friends.

BODY/HEALTH I'm in great shape, but if I had to be truly honest, I'm being a chicken about doing a triathlon. I keep saying I'm too busy to train, but the truth is I'm scared of the swim. But I suppose I should suck it up and do it, especially if I'm actually contemplating getting pregnant in the next year.

MONEY I'm being a jerk about money. I'd like to buy a condo but I keep buying myself these designer handbags and shoes because I think I deserve it. Plus I do it because when I face the reality that I need to be able to take care of myself, it makes me jealous of all my friends who have someone else who helps to support them. I shop as a way to not deal. It's stupid when I think about it. I need to get serious about my future and my savings.

Your turn:

1. Now ask yourself, in what areas of my life am I acting like a chicken? What am I too chicken to try?
2. Next ask yourself, in what areas of my life am I being a jerk? Describe how I act like a jerk including the things I say, do, or the attitude I have. Am I avoiding something? What am I angry about? Why am I being a jerk?

Learn to Recognize Fake Limits

Your brain is constantly producing propaganda to project a false sense of your personal limits. Think of it as an overeager natural defense system that is designed to protect you from stepping into situations that involve too much risk. You should never mistake your brain's messages for the actual truth about your ability to perform a task or as an accurate analysis of what the future will look like. Always remember that your wiring is very old, in evolutionary terms, and more than a little bit high-strung. Those signals are nothing more than warnings—and skewed warnings at that. The problem is, you listen to your brain and the propaganda it spews as if it is God talking. You must tune it out, if you want to turn on the powerful you.

Recent research highlights just how much your so-called limits are self-imposed. From the beginning of modern medicine, the working theory about physical exhaustion supposed that human limits were built into the body. According to the theory, the buildup of lactic acid in overworked muscles eventually killed their ability to function for too long. But researchers kept noticing anomalies that were hard to explain. People under extreme stress could far surpass their normal physical limits, and in other cases, the mentally ill might achieve world-record performances without any training. Clearly, the brain was playing a role.

In the 1990s a renegade notion arose that the brain has a central governor that monitors your body's energy supplies and burn rates. Its primary job is to keep your body from collapsing by artificially producing the sensation of muscle fatigue. This governor theory makes evolutionary sense. Animals whose brains safeguarded an emergency stash of physical reserves survived at a higher rate than animals that could drain their fuel tanks at will.

In other words, feeling tired is a trick launched by a small area in the front of the brain called the anterior cingulate cortex, to scare you into stopping. You've felt this a hundred times before. You are out for a jog, a long walk, or you simply decide to skip the elevator and opt for the three flights of stairs. In the beginning you feel strong, but at some point you'll start to feel tired and begin negotiating with yourself to slow down or stop. That's your brain cooking up some fake limits. You aren't really as tired as you feel; you can keep on going if you wanted to. This brain region regulates pain, emotion, and willpower. But like many things that the brain regulates, shifting attention away from its signals can defeat them. A purposeful distraction can defeat supposedly unendurable fatigue.

As one athlete who has excelled in extreme endurance biking

events puts it: "The pain doesn't exist for me. I know it is there because I feel it, but I don't pay attention to it. I sometimes see myself from the other view, looking down at me riding the bike. It is strange, but it happens like that." For us mere mortals, it can happen, too. If you can get a bigger mind-set for yourself and get out of the moment and look down on the situation, you'll be able to push through.

For our purposes, it simply comes down to recognizing the form these false mental limitations take, and making a decision to defy our feelings when they don't suit our purposes. Whether it is feeling like a chicken, acting like a jerk, feeling like a victim, or throwing a wet blanket on the future, you must recognize when the feelings kick in so you can defy them. The powerful you recognizes these feelings as false limits and doesn't pay attention to them. Knowing that your brain is spoofing you, there are times when you will need to push back. If you find yourself feeling "tired" or negative— distract yourself momentarily: play music, take a walk, leave the room—then refocus on the task at hand.

For an entire year, Ellen walked by the yoga studio and thought about taking a class. Ellen knew she was stuck. She stopped working when her daughter was born. Her days were soon consumed with sippy cups, diaper changes, nap schedules, playdates, and trips to the grocery. She wanted to find a way back to herself again. She wanted to find some meaning for herself and her life beyond "just being a mom." For an entire year, she made excuses. *I'll wait until she's two years old, then I can focus on me.* Finally, on a whim, Ellen decided that the time had come and walked into her first yoga class, accompanied by a more experienced friend.

It felt like a huge mistake. She started sweating the moment she walked into the room. She forgot a towel and water and felt really stupid about it. There was this chanting music playing that sounded cultish and made her uneasy. She laid out her mat in the back row and sat down like everyone else to wait for the class to start. She scanned the room. She was definitely the fattest one there. She wasn't wearing the "right" yoga workout clothes. She had on her old running shorts and a T-shirt over her jog bra. And within fifteen seconds of holding her first downward dog, her arms started shaking and the sweat rolled down her face and dripped off her nose into a pool on her mat. All she could think was, "What am I doing here? This is ridiculous. I'm going to have a heart attack."

For ninety minutes straight her brain screamed at her to leave. Her resistance was so loud she could barely hear the instructor cue the class. But she gritted her teeth, ignored her brain, and stayed on her mat. Trying to scare Ellen didn't work, so her brain started bargaining, "If that sweat pool expands so large that it spills over the edge of my mat and onto the studio floor, I'm out of here." When the sweat pool eventually reached the wood floor, she forced herself to stay until the end.

When the class ended just as it had begun, with three oms, she was too exhausted to even form the word. The friend who accompanied her to class leaned over and said, "Wasn't that great? You were awesome for a first timer! Want to go to class tomorrow?" She thought, "Are you trying to kill me?" But Ellen simply nodded yes.

Getting what you want never feels quite like you think it will. Resistance never goes away. A decade later, Ellen now owns her own yoga studio, but she still has days where she doesn't feel like it. Her mind still gives her a thousand reasons to bail. *You're tired. You practiced yesterday. You still have to hit the grocery store on the way home. You can do it tomorrow.* Resistance is always there. And like Ellen, your job is to always push through it.

Discover a *More Powerful You*

IN any area of your life that you want to change, adopt this rule. **Just do the things that you don't want to do.** Ellen didn't want to stay on that yoga mat. She didn't want to go back the next day. But she did it anyway. Alison didn't want to feel stage fright, but she auditioned anyway. Colleen didn't want to date a guy who was divorced, but she did it anyway. **If you only ever did the things you don't want to do, you'd have everything you've ever wanted.**

What's one area of your life that you want to change? List all the things you know you need to be doing, but (for whatever reason) don't feel like it.

_____

_____

_____

Good. Now be powerful: Do everything you just listed, even though you don't feel like it.

With practice you will get used to pushing through your bullshit excuses and resistant feelings; your mind and body will start to adapt to your newly expanded capacity to stretch yourself. You will become adept at what once felt difficult. Your mind will reset its limits, and little by little, your life will change and the powerful you will be in charge. The alarm bells won't go off quite as often, and it won't feel like a battle every time you try something new, hard, or scary.

It gets easier, but resistance never goes away completely. Ellen's resistance is alive and well and yours will be, too. She has just learned to ignore it and push through. Now it is your turn.

Pushing through your thoughts and feelings will be an enormous challenge. It's the emotional equivalent of trying to wake up from a dream. You will have to confront your own judgments, and power through the limitations, fatigue, and anti-actions your brain throws at you. It's the only way to get what you want in life.

Don't react to your feelings; become more powerful and dismantle them. A negative emotion gets in your face. It cuts to the front of the line in your mind and tries to elicit a reaction from you. It's like some annoying guy sitting next to you in a quiet café who is yammering on loudly. No matter how hard you try to concentrate on something else, his nasal voice forces you to pay attention.

When you're feeling a negative emotion creeping into your space, quickly dismantle it. You need to remind yourself that the negative emotion is an illusion, a bias against doing something different. Replace it with a positive action, which goes straight to the heart of your negativity. Just do the opposite of what you feel like doing. Say something to the loudmouth if normally you'd sit quietly, or don't say something and move your seat to another table if you'd usually be a jerk about it. **Breaking from your usual response will put you in the fast lane to discovering a more powerful you.**

It's hard to challenge your own feelings because you constantly normalize whatever you do, just because it's you who did it. You make whatever you're thinking now the baseline for good judgment, but the reality is that it's just one brain's opinion. Just because you thought it, doesn't mean it's a good idea. In fact, it usually isn't.

Pushing Through Is the All-Purpose Solution

Pushing through is the universal solution for dealing with feeling stuck. There is no point wallowing through the reasons for all the things that have slowed you down. No matter whether it is fear or anger that is slowing you down, you need to figure out what is going to advance your personal goals, and start taking action toward it. If you don't have what you want in one area of your life, defy your feelings and do what you must to get it.

Remember, all those feelings and doubts and concerns are nothing more than your brain's expression of the unknown. Your doubts are not a true, objective gauge of how good you really are at something. Your doubts are simply expressing your brain's concern that you haven't had lots of practice with the skills required for the task at hand. Whether it's fearing a confrontation with someone, or dreading a physically challenging task, your brain is declaring this activity unpleasant and avoidable. But that sure as heck is not the final verdict on whether it's doable. Once you learn that your brain has a bias toward keeping things the same, all those signals of discomfort are a much less compelling excuse.

There's another strong reason for overcoming your resistance—each time you push through, you're making a long-term investment in yourself. When you defy your resistance, you are broadening and building on your experiences. Unlike fear and caution, this is not an activity that is immediately rewarded by evolution. When you're cautious and manage to avoid a tiger in the jungle, that's an immediate reward. But when you broaden your range of experiences, and get more and more comfortable with new and challenging things, it has a powerful long-term effect. You are opening up the possibility for greater improvisation in your life in all sorts of new circumstances. Pushing yourself to read the business section at night, when you want to just veg out in front of the television, creates a well of knowledge in your mind that you might need to tap later. Reaching out and engaging with strangers despite your shyness will inject a new level of confidence and energy into your conversations that could pay off in an interview.

Michael is cleaning out the basement with his son. It's Saturday, and they're making piles of crap to take to the dump. "Hey, Dad, what's this?" His son starts to pick up a guitar case from beneath a pile of broken window shades. "The Melonheads?" he read from the sticker on its front. "What's that?"

Michael instantly remembers the band he formed with friends in high school, and wonders where everyone is now and thinks, "Gosh I should really start playing again . . ." He starts to think about his favorite riff, but he realizes that he's got to finish the basement by today, and they are way behind schedule. For a moment, he considers carrying the bass upstairs, but he hears his wife's footsteps upstairs as the baby starts crying again.

"Hey, put that back. I can play for you some other time. Mom will be furious if we don't finish this basement before the dump closes at three P.M." The moment is lost. Michael just convinced himself to stay the course and do nothing.

If he were to hold onto that momentary impulse, take some sort of small action to nurture it, and push through his internal resistance, his life would pivot. It would happen in small ways at first. He would stop sorting crap for twenty minutes, dust off the bass, and show his son a few riffs right then and there. Then he might just ban the TV after dinner and start playing again in the living room. His son might encourage him to go to an open-mic night or teach him how to play. Slowly, from that one moment, Michael's life could roll into a new direction. It would expand. Music would fill the empty spaces that a grinding job and demanding schedule had created inside of Michael. He had always thought he'd just do the lawyer thing, pay off his debt, stockpile some cash, and then pursue what truly interested him. But twenty years later, he's still toiling away at the firm. As the five seconds pass between his first impulse to play the bass and the decision to keep cleaning, the notes from the riff in his mind fade away.

Maybe your life took off quickly, too. You stepped into a job, maybe you got married, took on a mortgage, had some kids. No matter what your decisions, life got serious and expensive and you got stuck on the track you were on. Maintaining the rest of your life became your only job. You'd rather be doing something else with your life, but it seems impossible to make the transition and still pay the bills. So you just keep your head down. You shelved your dreams beside all the books you plan to read someday. The more you keep yourself glued to that narrow track, saying "maybe later" and "it's too late now" or "after I get done with this," the harder it is to force yourself to expand your life to include new areas.

But you need to stop saying no. Look where it's leading you. **The key to getting yourself unstuck is to start saying yes to those unexpected impulses that want to take you somewhere new.** Not only because it is the only way to relieve yourself of the monotony of life, but because of the other benefits to your mind and your happiness.

This isn't just common-sense wisdom. There's a whole body of research, led by Barbara Fredrickson from the University of North Carolina, that documents the long-term positive effects of "broaden and build" behavior. When you're asking yourself "why should I push through?" the answer is not merely that you're going to get something done that's going to make you feel better right now. You're also investing in your mind, broadening the range of experiences that still let you remain at ease, knocking down barriers that hold you back, and making sure that future forms of resistance will not slow you down so much. You're putting yourself in a position to move from surviving to thriving.

You might feel awkward. It's always going to feel uncomfortable doing something new. Standing on the stage, auditioning for *Rent,* Alison will feel a mix of elation and pride for pushing through and panic for being there. You're going to expose your own clumsiness and make mistakes. You're going to feel like you're faking it. None of that will matter when you get what you want. Pushing through means ignoring that voice that tries to dissuade you by making you feel ridiculous.

The truth is that people don't actually see as much of your faking as you believe. They tend to take you at face value. When you are making an effort, and people see you doing something that's difficult, they tend to overlook the mistakes. What they see is your effort. They assume that if you're doing it, then you've got some decent level of skill at it, or they envy and admire you for having the gumption to try.

Imagine you go to the doctor, and someone comes in to the exam room wearing a white coat. She is looking busy, smiles, and asks a few questions while looking through a nearby cabinet. Based on the situation, most people will assume it's the doctor, and actually start drawing some conclusions. They'll assume she's smarter and more professional than if she stepped in wearing a plain blue shirt. It's called cognitive dissonance, and it's what makes "fake it till you make it" such an effective strategy. When you give something a try, and you commit to it with your energy and attitude even though you feel nervous and awkward on the inside, people will pick up on your focus. Standing on a stage, attending a speed-dating event, or performing at open-mic night will feel like you are faking it. What's cool is that everyone else will actually tend to respect the fake part because you look like where you're supposed to be. That'll give the real you a chance to catch up.

It Takes a Lot of Work to Stay Stuck

Psychologists have learned that even our conscious decisions are heavily guided by our feelings and unconscious processes. Although you like to think you're in charge and your conscious, rational, objective mind is making all your decisions, the fact is that your unconscious mind tips the scales heavily. Even the thoughts we consider "conscious" and under our direct control have a lot of automatic thinking built into them. What's more, within this automatic thinking are a whole slew of distortions whose net effect, for our purposes, is to inhibit change. **So while one part of you has your eyes set on a dream, another part of your mind is actually battling *against* your dream.**

Just check out Brian. Every day is a battle. He starts each morning with a new resolution that he is going to put all his effort into being successful at his job, whether he likes it or not. By one in the afternoon, his mind is wandering. Another morning of witnessing incompetence and laziness has broken his resolution. He starts looking around for new jobs on Monster.com. After an hour, he decides to do some market research on new company ideas that he'd been toying with. Molly stops by and distracts him. He loses track of time staring at her leaning against the doorway to his office. Then the phone rings, and he starts worrying that he's slacking off too much. If he doesn't work harder, he'll get laid off. Back and forth until six, then he'll pack up and trudge home to Jennifer and the kids. Another day, and nothing has changed. His dream of starting a business and getting out of the mortgage industry is in mortal combat with his desire for stability.

At every step, there are unconscious feelings guiding you and battles being waged. Your mind is actively working against you and doing everything it can to thwart change. The more you deliberate and think about not following your dream, the more you're letting the bad guys win.

One of the clearest examples of your mind's effort to thwart change is caution. The same instincts that kept your ancestors on red alert—dodging tigers and avoiding poisonous snakes, keeping a weather eye on the clouds and worrying about what's hiding in the next bush—are still alive and well inside you. Caution has been one of mankind's greatest allies for a very long time, and your instincts are reluctant to give it up. The humans who stayed cautious and avoided taking unnecessary risks were obviously the ones who managed to stay alive long enough to pass along their genes. The feelings that signaled danger represented a safe limit for staying alive. It was your brain saying, "You can go this far, but no further." There was of course nothing stopping you from going further, and pushing through your fears, except the physical consequences of what might happen next. But today, when there are no tigers or poisonous snakes, having caution hardwired into the way you think is purely a liability.

Lisa walks into the office with a bag full of goodies. She's worked at the development office at Iowa State for the last three years and every holiday season, she gives her team the same gift: a gift card to iTunes and bag of homemade granola. Her assistant, Jessica, squeals with delight as Lisa reaches into the bag to give her the gift. "Oh my gosh, this better be your homemade granola! I wait all year for this stuff." Lisa laughs and hands her the little gift bag. Jessica rips open the top of the bag and digs her hand right into the toasted oats, coconut shavings, almonds, and pecan mix that is Lisa's famous homemade granola. With granola falling out of her mouth, Jessica says the sentence that Lisa has heard a thousand times from everyone who's tasted it. "You really should sell this stuff."

As soon as she hears the familiar phrase she hits the pause

button in her brain for just a second. She can envision herself in her kitchen, making batches of granola all day, classical music playing in the background and the dog at her feet. She imagines ditching the Theory suit for cargo pants, flip-flops, and tank tops. She'd have toned arms, exercise every morning after the kids got on the bus, and then spend the day baking granola. She thinks about the name for a second—3 Girl Granola (after her three little daughters)—and starts to envision the label. She's dreamed for years about getting out of the corporate world and doing something with cooking. For just a second, Lisa escapes her life and gets a glimpse of what she wants.

The pause button doesn't stick for long. Her brain has stepped in and started doing its thing. *Where would I sell it? Do I need a commercial kitchen? What would this cost me to produce? I can't afford to quit my job, how will I balance all this?* She is now entangled in caution and starts feeling chicken about the whole idea. Her head is spinning with obstacles, ideas, logistics, and fear and she pushes the idea right out of her mind.

Our cautious instincts worked great in the jungle, where there are hazards at every turn. But these calculations don't match the realities of the modern world. The same rules don't apply. As much as the nightly news may try to convince us that there's an abduction on every street corner, the fact is that modern life is simply not dangerous. Sure, you need to watch out for cars when you cross an intersection, but you really don't need to exercise as much caution as you think you do. If Lisa invests a hundred dollars to make a large batch of granola, print some labels, and show up at a farmer's market, the only thing she's risking is a C-note and a Saturday morning. It is risk free.

Another important thing to remember is that negative feelings talk louder in your brain. Chickens and jerks are loud. Caution has such importance from a survival perspective that hundreds of generations later, fear and worry have become your default settings. These negative feelings are designed to rise above and drown out other feelings. They have cognitive priority in your brain.

Will Lisa feel nervous driving over to the farmer's market on Saturday morning? Yes. Will she worry that the other vendors will be unwelcoming? Yes. Will she worry that her table will be vacant while the others have a line of customers four deep? Yes. Will any of this happen? Highly unlikely. If you're too busy picking flowers in the jungle, and your brain decides to ignore those worrisome footsteps sneaking up behind you, then you're simply not going to last too long. But too often you fail to remind yourself that no one is sneaking up on you at the farmer's market or in your basement on a Saturday morning. It's safe to sell some granola or strum a few chords for your son.

Discover a *More Powerful You*

WHAT'S something you've been thinking about doing for a while? Selling your spaghetti sauce? Writing a novel? Launching a business? Dating again? Signing up for a marathon? Moving to a new city? I guarantee you have placed limits on yourself and your idea. Perhaps you are willing to stick your neck out, but only so far. Lisa will make granola for friends but she won't try to make a business out of it. You will think endlessly about it, but not push through to action.

What do you want to try? _____

_____

What are the limits and excuses that your brain places on pursuing the idea? List them here (and make it as long as you like):

1. _____
2. _____
3. _____
4. _____

Now, become powerful: Find a way to take one small step forward. Hurry. The urge to act will disappear in five seconds.

That kind of prioritization—deciding which thoughts are important and which ones aren't—happens every day in your brain. The scientific term is *negativity bias*. It means that no matter where you are, your brain is like an emergency room on July Fourth weekend, and all the worst cases are always going to get the most attention. That's why when you're faced with a decision, worry and fear rise above most other feelings in your mind, even in a situation that mixes the good with the bad.

You need to take it on faith that if you weren't hardwired for the risks of the jungle, you might feel differently about taking a risk and following your dream. There's no easy way around feeling like a chicken. You just need to perform a kind of manual override, and stick up for the feelings of adventure, accomplishment, and progress that are getting beat up and drowned out by your negativity bias. You need to help them get on their feet.

Let's go back to the moment when Jessica is pumping fistfuls of that granola into her mouth and says, "You should sell this stuff." If Lisa were to override the caution and say, "You know, Jessica, you are the hundredth person who has said that to me. I'm going to stop being a chicken and do it," that would change everything.

Instead of standing there lost in thought wondering, "Should I do this or not?" and slowly starving the impulse, she would feed the impulse by speaking it and let it have a chance to become a reality.

"Jessica, will you help me do it? I need you. I need you to push me. Just be a pain in the ass and ask me every day what I've done, okay? And yell at me when I start slacking off."

"If it means I'll get free granola, I'll show up here every morning in a pair of high black boots with a whip to crack."

What happened in those five seconds is critical. Lisa reversed the flow of energy in her mind. Instead of the thought disappearing and retreating toward caution, she pushed it through her brain, out her mouth, and spoke it into taking action. Is she done? Of course not. She'll have to push through every single moment she feels caution rise up to stop her. That's the definition of being powerful. This is just the beginning of Lisa getting to pursue her dreams. But without this moment, and without this "take action" muscle getting worked, there is nothing.

It's time to reconsider your limits. In the modern world, fear is baggage. You need to question all those feelings and signals that your unconscious mind is sending you. Caution keeps you from making a change. Worry stops you from taking action. Uncertainty prevents you from exploring and breaking out of your routines. Anxiety inhibits you from taking even the most basic risks.

These feelings are just evolutionary baggage. They don't represent a clear, objective limit. To break out of these patterns, you need to examine the way you think. You need to see how fear and caution mess with your mind and make you avoid risks, or invent risks where they don't really exist.

You must break out of your personal ruts so you can truly and honestly feel happy and satisfied with your life. Finding meaning and purpose in your life is the "new survival." This means breaking away from that caution that colors your mind. Nine times out of ten, when you feel caution, there is no risk. It's your evolutionary hard-wiring peering into the darkness and saying, beyond this point lies the unknown, and the unknown should be feared. But the unknown shouldn't be feared. It should be embraced. **Feeling nervous is not a red flag warning you of danger. Nerves mean you are about to do something *NEW*! Feeling nervous is part of the program, so expect to feel nervous! It is a signal to step on the gas, not the brake.**

Status Quo Bias

Another bias in our thinking circles around loss and status quo. Psychologists have studied different forms of this bias and given them a variety of names—*endowment effect, loss aversion, pseudocertainty bias*—but basically they boil down to the fact that people hate to lose things. We are all obsessed with hanging onto what we've got, at any price.

Studies have proven that all humans have this weakness. Once you own something, and it's in your possession, you artificially inflate its value in your mind. It's like the classic "bird in the hand, worth two in the bush," but it goes even further. Once you've got that bird in your hand, and despite all evidence to the contrary, you will firmly and devoutly believe that your bird is better than any other bird around. Period. Anyone who has ever picked out one puppy from a litter of nearly identical ones knows exactly what I'm talking about.

Trial periods and rebates exploit this fact to lock in better sales. By putting something into your hands, and starting to make you feel like you own it, you're inevitably going to pay more than you would have originally paid up front, just so they don't take it away. It's been proven in experiment after experiment that we're suckers for that kind of stuff. And this goes way beyond letting go of physical things. We have trouble letting go of how we spend our day, our habits, our routines, and even the relationships that make us miserable.

You see, when you really dig into the feelings underlying these biases, it turns out that loss aversion and the endowment effect are not about the *things* we own. They're about the feeling of loss. We hate to lose, and we go to great lengths to avoid the feeling of losing something. This hardwired bias is extremely powerful and it completely colors our view of the world.

The crazy part is *how much* excess value we attach to something that we wouldn't have cared about earlier, and *how much* you'll do to avoid losing it. Once it's yours, you become so fixated on keeping it that you'll do much more to keep it than you would have ever done to acquire it in the first place.

Simply because it's yours, you think it's way more valuable, and it's going to take a lot more money and convincing for you to give it up. It's been proven that people consistently and constantly make the same choices over and over, just because they're scared to lose something.

The problem is that when you overvalue what you have—whether it's a puppy, a car, a job, or a relationship—you are already unconsciously against any kind of change that would risk losing that thing. As a result, when it comes to making a change, your motivations are totally skewed and you can't see straight. Any change is going to involve some sacrifice. You've got to take a hard look at something you've got right now—whether it's something material or a lifestyle or a feeling—and give it up.

Because you have got a serious case of "status quo bias," you're going to feel especially reluctant to make that sacrifice. No matter what you're getting in return, giving up anything is going to feel wrong. Your brain will be screaming, "Don't risk it! Don't risk the loss!"

But I'm here to tell you that most of that feeling is a distortion. It's a totally irrational bias. You need to understand that your aversion to change is wrong. It's a piece of reflex thinking.

I see it play out in all sorts of ways every day. People go to ridiculous lengths to preserve a status quo, even when they can't stand it. For example, if you are struggling to lose weight, you are trying to hold onto your freedom to eat whatever the hell you want. Often you will make more effort to preserve the status quo than what it would take for a change. That's crazy. If you examine your own actions you'll start to see the same status quo bias. And typically you are so bloody stubborn about being told what to do that you are a complete jerk about changing it.

At least once a week, someone will call into the radio show because her marriage isn't working and she wants some advice. A complaint I hear all the time from men and women of all ages is what I call the "roommate syndrome." Robert Reich refers to this phenomenon as "double-income no sex" or DINS in his book *Aftershock*. Regardless of the name, it is a serious problem in relationships today.

Stephanie is in just such a relationship. Over time, the sex with her husband has disappeared and the couple has essentially become roommates. The distance between them grows every day, but when you press her, she ferociously defends the miserable situation. She'll do anything and fight any fight to hang onto what she's got.

Dear Mel,

I haven't had sex with my husband in at least six years. (We have been married for twenty-one years.) I have tried countless times to discuss it, but no improvement. On the surface our relationship looks good and I appear happy. As you may have guessed, this is just the tip of the iceberg. I think

I am depressed about everything and can only remember how
excited I used to be about life.

   I am now thinking about what life will be like when my
two daughters (sixteen, fourteen) go off to college. I want to
get a job, but realize that when I left my job sixteen years ago
to raise my children (I wanted to do this), I left my successful
career in ashes. I am capable and have a lot of skills, but just
can't seem to focus on a new career. If I could earn some money
I think I would feel better about myself.

   I don't know if I should leave my husband, Aaron, to
find the physical relationship I want. In this note, I think it
is pointless to begin a litany of my husband's great qualities,
which are many; most everything about him is wonderful.
Most things I confront him with and discuss lead to insight
and thus changes in both of our behaviors, which is great. But
the sex thing really bugs me.

   My self-confidence is shredded, I need a style makeover,
and feel the need to create something (job). I am beginning to
feel angry about a lot of things in my relationship, rightly or
wrongly.

   I would like to talk to someone with your insight and
hear a new perspective. I am a get-it-done type of person but
just don't know what to get done.

   Can you help me?

This is the classic "heart of gold" argument that is a sure sign
of status quo bias. I hear it constantly. "Sure, the marriage is broken
and I'm miserable, but he's really got a heart of gold." Despite a
basic and fundamental flaw in the relationship, the unhappy person
finds every possible excuse for her spouse. Underneath the woe-is-me
"get-it-done" gal is a pissed-off woman who is feeling angry, hurt,

and insecure but refuses to leave or take any kind of meaningful action to change it.

No wonder Stephanie feels paralyzed. She's locked into a mental tug-of-war with herself. What's most striking is her willingness to shut up and put up. It takes an enormous amount of effort and pretending and make-believe to keep up appearances. She's completely pissed off and miserable. Her self-confidence is shredded. But she works hard to maintain the status quo "for the kids"— even though everyone in the household is miserable and walking on eggshells.

Reading her e-mail, you can imagine how her day-to-day routine ground her life to a halt. You can imagine that she and her husband have settled into their routine with each other. It's how their marriage has survived this long. They lead separate lives by day, because he's off at work and she is focused on their two daughters. Aaron "has to" travel a lot for work, but they both know it's just easier when he spends the week on the road. When Aaron is home he feels like a guest in someone else's house. Petty fights dominate the weekends and she's constantly on his case for leaving the toilet seat up, the dishes in the sink, and sleeping in too late. All of which he does precisely to annoy her.

The idea of sex at this point is a joke. They can't stand each other anymore. He's always the first to bed and is sound asleep by the time she arrives. That's fine with her. They act like roommates, which is why they feel like roommates. Of course, that won't stop her from thinking and analyzing and contemplating and complaining. She could spin for years, happily expending all her effort to preserve something that's making her miserable—because she won't take the risk of losing what she's got. And what does she have? A crappy marriage and two kids who knew years ago that their parents are miserable.

Waiting around for something to change will slowly kill you. Wouldn't it be great if Aaron just woke up one day and was the same guy Stephanie fell in love with two decades ago and her anger was gone? Wouldn't it be wonderful if her old boss from sixteen years ago called and said he needed her back? Yes, it would. That would be amazing. But it is not happening unless you fight for it.

You need to hear this loud and clear: *No one is coming.* **It is up to you.** It has always been and will always be up to you. You may never feel inspired or clearheaded enough to seize a moment, but you have to force yourself to do it even if you don't want to. *Nothing is changing unless you make it change.*

Discover a *More Powerful You*

HOW long have you been waiting for someone in your life to change? Who is it? Your partner? Your boss? Your mom?

Who is it?_____

How long have you been waiting? _____

How long have you been waiting to be happy?

_____

How long have you been waiting for the right job, the right lover, the right diet to simply show up?

_____

Aren't you tired of waiting? Become powerful: Pick one small thing you can commit to doing to reverse the direction this is all headed in, and *do it*.

Hurry, within five seconds the impulse to act will start to disappear.

The best time to act on a feeling you have is right now. Thinking about it just makes it harder. Remember the five-second rule. The moment you are worried about your relationship, tell someone and ask him or her to help you. If you are waiting until the kids go to college before you deal with your lousy marriage, don't wait. If you are waiting until after the holidays to start your diet, start it right now. If you are waiting to figure out what to do with your life until you have more time, make the time to start your search right now. The longer you wait, the less likely you will act.

You Don't Have a Clue How Great
Your Life Could Be

A third great example of how your unconscious bias undercuts you is your inability to accurately forecast the future. You'd think that humans are pretty good at that stuff. We're the only species with a prefrontal cortex. This is the chunk of brain that keeps us number one in the food chain, and where our imagination is stored. The prefrontal cortex lets us imagine, with surprising vividness—even if we've never seen or experienced it—things like pickle ice cream, or a baseball game in space, or a cat singing "Happy Birthday."

You'd expect that such a powerful tool could help you plan for the future. Just by putting together a few basic ideas, your mind can actually project into the future and start imagining the results. For example, as you start picturing and plotting your next move, whether it's graduating from college, applying to the Culinary Institute of America, or confronting your passive-aggressive coworker, you'd expect the prefrontal cortex could help you imagine how you'll feel when you achieve it.

Don't count on it. Despite what you believe, you can't predict well at all. Hundreds of research experiments have proven that your brain consistently overestimates how bad something will make you feel. As a result, you never feel as bad as you expect when things go wrong.

For example, when you try to imagine how you'd feel after a nasty divorce, or losing your job, or rejection after an audition, you will categorically imagine the worst. Whether you think you're going to be crushed and depressed for weeks, or crying hysterically for days, you'll be exaggerating. Research has proven that it's never as bad as you think.

Think about what a handicap that is when you're trying to get fired up to make a change. When you think about a change in your life, you line up all the bad parts into a giant wall of pain: Tell Aaron you want a divorce. Have a huge fight. Cry a lot. Upset the kids. Disappoint your parents. Hire a lawyer. Live through the anger and the tension. Spend too much money. Feel heartbroken. Console the kids. Lose the house. Lose custody. Die a spinster. Regret it for the rest of your life.

Simultaneously, your brain also creates a skewed prediction of what your life will be like if you *don't* change. **Because your brain would prefer that you remain stuck, it tells you that staying stuck is always safe.** If you don't ask for that divorce, you might not find true love, but at least you'll always have stability, right? If you don't leave the job you hate, at least you'll always have a steady paycheck, right? But this is just as skewed a perspective as your worst-case-scenario predictions about change are. The truth is that even if you don't ask for that divorce, your spouse could. Just because you don't leave that job doesn't mean it will be there forever. Not going to the gym might mean you avoid feeling embarrassed about your weight in the short term—but what happens next time you're invited to go to the beach? Your brain tries to tell you that change is dangerous, and that staying stuck is safe. But the truth is that not only is change not as dangerous as your brain insists, staying stuck isn't half as safe as it predicts it will be.

Notice that when your brain predicts the awful consequences of change or the absolute safety of staying stuck, your brain is not actually telling you what to do. Instead it's *framing* the event in a way that makes change depressing and fearful. It's stacking the deck against change, so that you can feel as if you made the decision yourself, but in truth the frame made the decision for you. That biased frame is the enemy. To get what you want, you must ignore it.

What makes us so bad at forecasting how we'll feel? First of all, when we create a mental snapshot of our future, we fill it with one-sided visions. This is called *focalism.* We focus only on the primary event that we're predicting. We imagine looking for a job and think almost exclusively about all the difficulties we'll encounter. We don't build a balanced picture that combines the good with the bad.

Picture the scenes of you getting laid off: You're getting the bad news, you're packing your cube into a box, you're breaking it to your family, you're desperately reading the want ads, you're standing in long lines, you're getting rejected, your money is running out, you're pulled over on the highway and crying alone in the car.

Everyone's brain does this, which is why so many become trapped by their worst-case-scenario projections. Alison pictures her neck rash and rejection. Colleen has concluded she's a spinster. Lisa is afraid she won't be able to pay the mortgage selling granola. Michael feels as if the slightest deviation from his routine will somehow jeopardize everything he's built. These projections convince you that taking action is useless—so you don't.

Inevitably, when imagining the future you'll also leave out all the good stuff. What about all the support you'll get? What about your kids seeing you try to start a business? What about thirty-nine weeks of unemployment? What about not having to commute to a job you hated? What about strengthening your marriage by working as a team to tighten the budget and get your priorities straight? What about discovering what you want to do with your life? What about your friends rallying to help? What about joy? Life really does keep moving, and it's got a way of smoothing the edges.

The second reason we're so bad at emotional forecasts is that we underestimate the power of what researchers call our *psychological immune system*. We forget all the coping mechanisms that we constantly use to fight off pain and mental suffering. There's all sorts of chemistry in our brains that takes the edge off bad news. We synthetically produce happiness, and that lets us more easily cope with difficult times.

The first few days might be hell. But a few good nights' sleep and some exercise dulls the blow of most bad news. The passing of time truly heals any wound. We can fight off sadness and depression much better than we realize.

Step outside your mental snapshots. Step outside your habits of framing the future as a worst-case scenario, and imagining every possible "what-if." The worst is never as bad as you think. My grandfather always used to say, when we rode in his boat and I would worry out loud about capsizing or sinking or any number of unlikely scenarios, "Anything can happen, Mel, but it usually doesn't."

Our eleven-year-old received the birthday party invitation in the mail from her best friend. She opened it up and had a blank expression on her face. "Paint ball?" "It's coed?" "It's outside in the woods?" "We hold real guns?" "What if I get hurt?" "Who's on my team?" For days she debated whether or not to go to the party. I could see her trying her best to push herself through her fears, her excuses, and her resistance. But every day, she had new questions and concerns. I wouldn't have been thrilled about the idea either, but I didn't tell her.

The day of the party, when it was time to leave, she burst into tears and ran up to her room. Her resistance had won. That's where she would have stayed if she were an adult. Luckily for her, she's only eleven and she still has a parent like me to bully her past her fears and into the car. She cried the whole way to the party. When we pulled into the driveway, ten kids were standing around waiting for her to arrive so they could leave for the paint ball field.

She sucked back the tears, got out of the car, and sheepishly walked over to the four other girls who were standing off to the side. I heard one of them scream, "Sawyer, I'm so glad you are here! I'm terrified!" "So am I. I almost didn't come!" said Sawyer. She had just pushed through her resistance by admitting it.

When I picked her up five hours later, her clothes were splattered with paint and she was exhilarated and talking a mile a minute. "The guns were huge! Check out my hand, I got pegged right here by Jeremy and it still hurts. Kate hit Chris in the head and he started bleeding! Mr. Craig was amazing—he tagged everyone!" On and on she went about the day in the woods, firing paint balls at boys, taking hits and ducking for cover. Underneath the enthusiasm I could hear something even cooler than an eleven-year-old who had just had a great time—she felt proud of herself.

Whether you're eleven years old or forty, when you start worrying, it doesn't mean anything is going to go wrong. It just means you are about to try something new. The only thing to do when the what-ifs come is to push through. **Being powerful doesn't mean the what-ifs disappear, it means you ignore them and move forward.**

New things don't feel safe. They make the forecasting engine in your mind go haywire. The only thing that feels safe to your mind is what you already know—being stuck (and even that isn't as safe as your mind would like to believe). Your mind will trick you into expending enormous amounts of energy keeping you stuck. By stewing over what-ifs, you're taking time and energy away from much more productive pursuits. It takes effort to avoid conversations. It takes effort to feel stressed out. It takes effort to cycle through what-ifs and torture yourself with worry.

The bottom line is that you've got a huge number of internal forces that are working to screw you to the rails of life. That's why it is essential that you get your desires out of your head. You must speak them out loud like Lisa did when she asked Jessica to help her finally do something about her granola. Then take action immediately before that brain of yours smashes it back into dust. And once you speak it and start taking action, you need to know how the world today works so you can keep pushing yourself forward, no matter what rises up to stop you.

CHAPTER THREE

Routines

Why Your Freedom Depends on Breaking Them

These days everyone feels a bit blah, bored, or burned by life. The majority of people can't stand their jobs; we are getting fatter every year, working more, and sleeping less; and our overall happiness is declining. Our grandparents and parents never sat around bemoaning the moments they felt stuck in life—it wasn't even on their radar screen. But modern life has a way of getting you stuck. There are three primary factors behind our widespread modern malaise: choice, uncertainty, and routine. Anytime you start feeling overloaded with choices, overwhelmed with uncertainty, or locked into an inescapable routine, you become stuck. So let's take a closer look at each trigger and how it shuts down your impulse to take action.

Too Many Choices Overheat Your Mind

The first problem with life today is what many still consider its biggest strength. We live in a society where you can have pretty much anything. And that's the way it should be. In a democratic society, we all believe that freedom translates into the power to choose. We can choose what we watch, what we hear, what we do, and what we think.

But something happened along the way. The power to choose has exploded into something that's overpowering and that actually undermines our mental well-being. A quick trip down any supermarket aisle will demonstrate the problem. Why do we need to decide between thirty types of mustard, hundreds of different cereals, and dozens of types of chocolate chip cookies?

Go to any electronic store and try to figure out what kind of DVD player you need. Try to sort out which health plan you should choose, what doctor, what dentist. It's a nightmare. We are faced with an ever-multiplying, bewildering number of choices. I'm sure there are plenty of economists who could explain why choice is important and how it increases competition and diversity. But something has gone wrong when I have to decide among fifteen different varieties of potato chips. I remember when there were three flavors—plain, barbecue, and salt and vinegar. That felt easy. But these days, choosing is never easy.

We're supposed to somehow be benefiting from all the choices that we've been given, but half the time they just make us feel terrible. Researchers have proven that too many choices lead to confusion and unhappiness. How many times have you wavered over a decision at a restaurant because there are so many different plates to choose from that you can't make up your mind? Only with the waiter breathing down your neck do you finally pick something. It took that kind of pressure to break you out of analysis paralysis. And that's when you're picking something simple! So when your choice will have a larger impact on your life it's no wonder you don't have a clue which choice you should make.

In fact, when you're faced with too many options, many times you'll simply choose not to decide. In a classic social psychology experiment, researchers set up two different displays of gourmet jam on different days at the same supermarket. One arrangement presented twenty-four different varieties of jam, and the other only presented six different jams. Each display offered free samples and a discount coupon on whatever jam a customer might choose. The results were surprising, and tell us a lot about how choice operates on our minds.

Far more people were attracted to the twenty-four-jam display. More than 60 percent of passersby were drawn in to taste a sample, but in the end, only 3 percent actually purchased a jam. In contrast, while only 40 percent of passersby sampled the six-jam display, 30 percent made a purchase. Choice overload killed decision making.

Think about it for a second. We supposedly want more choices, and our first reaction when we see more choices is to swoop in excitedly. More choice means more fun! So cool! Let's try all those jams! But very quickly we're overloaded. Our brain gets woozy trying to weigh the merits of boysenberry-rhubarb compared to blackberry-peach—never mind raspberry-currant. Within a few moments it's all a blur, and we just walk away. Faced with too many choices, we choose not to decide.

But the unhappiness that is associated with choice goes deeper. Research experiments demonstrate that too many choices create a feeling of regret. When we have too many choices, no matter what we decide we later think about all the options we left behind. Even if you were happy with your choice, the knowledge that you could have chosen differently makes you start to wonder if you missed out by not choosing something else. When you think about what to do with your life, this can be paralyzing.

Tanya graduated from Marymount University with a degree in

dance. Now she's back home, living in her childhood bedroom and feeling completely lost. The world is so big. There are endless opportunities but none feel as if they're open to her. She always knew what to do next in life until right now: go to elementary school, then middle school, then high school, then take the SATS, apply for college, and go to the best school she could.

Now she has no clue what to do with her life and is confused and scared. She's working at her dad's restaurant as a hostess. One night a friend from high school comes in. "Tanya? What are you doing here? I heard you were a dancer in NYC."

Standing there in her dumb apron and Sunshine Diner T-shirt, she just wants to disappear. So she lies. "Dad needed my help for a couple of weeks, so I came home."

For the first time in her life, Tanya feels as if all her friends have pulled ahead of her and left her in the dust. She can fill ketchup bottles at the end of the night, but what else can she do? She feels like a tiny piece of plankton in a huge ocean. Walking into the Career Services office at school, the choices of what path to take just felt overwhelming, and now she's second-guessing all her decisions. "Should I follow my friends to Crested Butte for the winter and try to get a job?" "Do I keep applying for internships?" "Should I go back to New York and sleep on Sarah's couch and go to auditions?" "How do I get started in the real world?"

To become powerful, Tanya just needs to pick something. There is no "right" choice and there is no "wrong" choice. What Tanya is missing is that no matter what direction she picks, there is no real risk. As soon as she makes a choice, she will stop spinning and she will move forward. Tanya feels stuck because her life isn't moving anywhere. So all she has to do to get unstuck is simply pick a direction. She'll feel it out for a bit and if she doesn't like it, she can explore something different. Eventually she'll bump into the right path.

When you don't know what to do, just do the first thing that pops in your mind, *especially* if it's scary. There's a brand-new field of study around "emerging adulthood," and the early findings show that human beings require this phase of self-growth and exploration for our brains to fully mature. You need to explore for your brain to mature and continue to grow new cells.

If, for example, Tanya moves to Crested Butte she'll be doing something important—taking action, trying something new, living in a different part of the country, meeting new people, and most important, she'll stop spinning. It is another argument supporting the "you never know where this will lead" theory of change. You never know what will happen when you make a choice. She could spend the season working the chairlift with the son of the CEO of Sony. That could lead to an internship that she's always dreamed of. Or maybe it won't. But if she hates it, she can just move back home and fill ketchup bottles again until she picks the next thing to try.

Making a change in our lives requires making decisions and choices. If we're constantly battling the confusion of too many choices, and the regret of making the wrong choices, we are going to be feeling less confident and less open to choosing a course of action. We are going to become stuck. If you are in the same boat as Tanya and can't figure out the "right" thing to do with your life, then the solution is to stop ruminating and pick *something*.

Discover a *More Powerful You*

IF you are paralyzed with indecision like Tanya, you now know what you need to do. Don't worry about making the right decision, just make a decision.

> The paralysis is what's making you feel stuck. Research shows that it takes between twenty-one and thirty days for a new habit to kick in and feel right. So give whatever decision you make a good go for at least four weeks. If it doesn't feel right after trying it out for four weeks, then just pick a new direction.

When Uncertainty Strikes, Your Brain Retreats

A second reason that getting stuck has become a social epidemic is the increasing level of uncertainty in our lives. Uncertainty keeps you from trying new things, moving faster, or even moving at all. When you feel uncertain, you become stuck.

The economic crisis has put a strain on everyone. But the problem goes much deeper than just the past few years. Over the past several decades, life has gotten steadily more expensive for middle-class families, even though a second wage earner has entered the workforce. For everyone but the richest Americans, wages in relation to the cost of living have steadily declined since 1980, and families are much more likely to see a major disruption in their income stream. All of this financial pressure robs you of confidence about the future, and that uncertainty reduces risk taking. This results in more and more people getting stuck.

We can all relate to that feeling. The numbers assure us that it's not just our family that's not saving any money. We're all putting our debt onto credit cards. We're all coming up short at the end of the month. No one is socking anything away. With that kind of atmosphere, the notion of starting a new business or financing an education is not the happiest topic at the dinner table. When you've got such little margin for error in your monthly budget, you're going to feel a lot less adventurous about taking a financial chance on some new idea if it's going to come back and bite you later. So you put off your dreams for another year.

When Brian raised the idea of starting a business three years ago, Jennifer peppered him with questions about health care, the type of business he wanted to open, and the cost, and suggested that maybe he should just go back into sales. Clearly she wasn't onboard, so he didn't raise it again.

One thing to remember when uncertainty strikes is that while it's true that there is no way to predict what will happen if you take a risk, it's just as true that there is no way to predict what will happen if you *don't* take a risk. Not starting a business doesn't mean Brian is safe, even if it feels that way. He could be laid off, or his job could relocate. The idea that staying stuck is keeping him safe is an illusion. No matter what you do, life will have surprises in store. The difference is that when you make a positive change, you are choosing to take on the uncertainty of life on your own terms.

You Are Addicted to Your Routines

Perhaps the biggest reason you are so stuck is simply because you are used to it. Modern life throws so many choices and so much uncertainty at you that it feels like the only way to cope is by spending all of your energy keeping your life in a comfortable routine, even though it's not making you happy. You instinctively value familiarity over the risk of change, and unsurprisingly, you become dissatisfied. Maybe you've got your "being single" routine, or your "just another workday" routine, or your "my friends are boring, but I don't have any others" routine.

When you're locked into a routine, there's nothing exciting heading your way. It's just the same old boring stuff, day in and day out. But as much as you may want a change, the truth is that you feel comfortable in your routine, even if it isn't making you happy.

Take Kathy, for instance. Back in high school, Kathy was voted "Most Likely to Succeed," "Teacher's Pet," and half of the "Cutest Couple." She met Ron in college. She felt totally lost in the sea of students at the big state school so she threw herself into the relationship instead of her studies. The baby came first, and then they got married. Ron started working for his father's insurance business out of college and Kathy stayed home. At some point she just stopped thinking about what she wanted from life and figured that this was it.

By the time she turned thirty-five she and her husband had grown completely apart, and she'd become miserable. Deep down, she was afraid of leaving him and trying to make it as a single mom. So she just focused on surviving. Before long she had become comfortable with her own unhappiness. Like Stephanie, she could only remember how excited she used to be about life. If she just kept her head down and got lost in a routine of housework and daily chores, she could force herself to forget that life had anything more to offer. Occasionally a great novel or movie would make her start to think about other possibilities. But it didn't last long. She lost the ability to step outside of her routine and see all that life had to offer.

It's easy to become like Kathy and start to think that your routine is all there is to your life. You forget that there's anything more than what you've got. You wake up at the same time, brush your teeth with the same hand, dress in generally the same style, eat largely the same breakfast, fix your coffee a specific way, commute to work the same way, and on and on. Obviously, routines are a requirement in daily life, but they're a devil's bargain. They automate our brains, structure our lives, and make things easier, but in return they rob our day of variety and creativity. They erase any sense of exploration. There's nothing that can make you feel quite so robotic as a routine.

Of course, if every day was an adventure, and every morning required remastering how to make coffee and toast, you'd never make it to work before noon. By removing a set of activities from the foreground of thinking, you can free up mental real estate for other things. You turn the boring stuff into a series of habits, characterized by cold efficiency and lack of awareness. But in that bargain, everything you commit to routine is a theft. Sure, you imprint a repeatable activity into your mind, so you hardly think about it anymore. But at the same time, you lose the richness of an experience just for the sake of just getting it done.

When you're stuck, you've taken it too far. You channel yourself into a routine that submerges any sense of difference between days. You've had that experience where you arrive at work and don't quite remember getting yourself there. Taking the same path to work every day creates what scientists call a "stable environment" that promotes automated thinking. That kind of routine can be as hard to shake as a cigarette addiction: You want to quit the habit but there are too many situational cues and the path in your mind is well worn and just too easy to go down.

In fact, the same zone in your brain that lets you create mental routines in your life is also responsible for the automatic behaviors associated with addiction and compulsion. The formation of every habit in your life can be isolated to a small region of the brain called the basal ganglia. This little walnut-size area is where behaviors are transformed into routines, and addictions get formed. The common origin of routines and addictions offers a tantalizing clue to the persistence of routine in your life.

This zone functions by recognizing something in the outside world, which we'll call the trigger, and telling your mind what your next action should be in order to deliver a positive result. In the case of addiction, you see a cigarette (or a cup of coffee, or an actor, or a billboard, or anything else you've associated with cigarettes) and you feel an immediate compulsion to smoke, because you know from a whole series of past actions that smoking a cigarette delivers the nicotine buzz. Your brain has already built a direct shortcut from trigger to reward. The strength of these compulsions can be very hard to fight. Many extremely reputable scientists would say that addiction is outside your conscious control, even though the whole process occurs in your own brain, because it never really enters your conscious thoughts. The decision making is happening elsewhere.

And correspondingly, routine is like a kind of miniaddiction to your daily life from which you can't break free. Your brain keeps clicking back into old modes, trigger-to-reward, sparked by the repetition of all the same cues you experience every day. Every time you fire up the coffeemaker, start the car, turn on the computer, or grab the remote, your brain feels compelled to stick with its routine. In a familiar environment, your brain will always feel compelled to pursue the routines that you've already built. In many ways, your everyday routines are really little more than diluted forms of addiction, which is what makes breaking out of them so tough. It requires a level of vigilance to really think about what you're doing when you're in a routine.

Harold has been a smoker for thirty-seven years. There were decades of his life where he just loved to smoke. The cigarette he enjoyed while driving the car tasted like freedom, each puff took him somewhere far away. The first one in the morning before he brushed his teeth slowly coaxed him out of bed. He'd reach for the cigarettes before he even sat up. He felt invincible lying there—as if everything he had before him was actually doable. The cigarette he enjoyed while watching the ball game made the experience even more pleasurable.

But these days smoking doesn't add an extra rush to life. Forking over the astronomical price for a pack is irritating. Standing outside the office building in the rain makes him angry. He hates the fact that he's a smoker. He doesn't enjoy the act itself, and he doesn't like the way he smells, especially around his grandkids. He wishes he could quit. He thinks about it all the time, but he can't. Every time he encounters one of the triggers that he associates with smoking—like driving, waking up, watching the game—he gets a fierce craving. It's just more comfortable to keep smoking, even though he hates it.

Any area of your life can become like Harold's smoking. You want to change it, but it feels like too much work. But that's the rub. Releasing the brake on your mind *will* take work. The first time Harold wakes up and there's no pack of cigarettes on his nightstand to complete his morning routine, his brain will start screaming at him. He'll break into a cold sweat. He'll think, "I should run down to 7-Eleven. This is the dumbest idea. I can't do this!" He will hunt through the house and every coat pocket, check under the car seats to see if there's any errant cigarette rolling around. And when he stands up from the frenzy, pushes through, and pops a piece of crappy-tasting Nicorette into his mouth, he will have stalled the emotional storm for about five minutes until he encounters his next trigger. To quit, Harold has to push through the emotional storm. People quit smoking every day because they take power over their brains. You may be saying, "Hey. Wait a minute, Mel, nicotine is as physically addictive as heroin. It's not just mind over matter." The fact is, yes it is. Yes your body will crave it—quitting means being more powerful than the addiction. The same is true of your addiction to negative thoughts and ways of doing things.

When you try to break apart a routine you've had for a long time, expect to fight against yourself, especially when you encounter triggers and situational cues that push you back toward your old habits.

Your life is made up of a series of small moments and decisions. If you become numb to the small stuff, then that's why your life isn't changing. **Something as small as the urge to play the bass guitar, the impulse to show up at an audition, or the whim to walk into a yoga class can change your life if you act on it.** And yet you keep ignoring those impulses, tuning out those urges, or dismissing those whims as if they don't matter. And the fact is, they are everything. Each one of those small moments is a little point of leverage that you can use to create a true change. True momentum doesn't come from a blanket decision to change your life from top to bottom in one fell swoop. Momentum is a cumulative force that rolls our lives forward in small, but new directions. True momentum builds from all the tiny flickers of engagement and uncertainty that you discover and create in your day.

These moments are something to look forward to and keep watch for. Recognizing and seizing these moments is like opening a doorway into an alternate universe where your life is not governed by routine. Each moment that you recognize and act upon moves you toward something else that you can look forward to. They occur in our lives all day long. Yet, over and over, we don't take them.

Last year, a guy called into my radio show with a deep, seductive baritone voice. Gerald was fifty-seven years old and I almost dropped the microphone when he explained that he had been addicted to heroin, cocaine, and weed for thirty-nine years of his life. He blew a promising career in basketball, dropped out of college, and managed to get by working as an electrician for Amtrak. Eventually he bottomed out and found himself in and out of jail and living on the streets of New York City underneath the very same tracks he used to repair as an electrician. I explained that there was nothing to do but get sober, that he needed professional help, and to stay on the line so I could connect him with my producer, who would help him get a number to a program in his area. He responded, "No ma'am, I don't need detox. I'm sober. I have been for nine years."

Gerald went on to say that he had realized how much work it was taking to stay on drugs. He was a hustler. Whatever he needed for those thirty-nine years—money, drugs, sex—he could always hustle and get it. Until one day he woke up in the bed of some junkie he had met the night before. After doing heroin together at her apartment, he slept most of the day and woke up in the late afternoon sweaty and disoriented. He'd been in this situation hundreds of times, but on this day, he did something small and it changed his life. He had what recovering addicts call "a moment of clarity" and admitted the truth to himself. He admitted that he was tired of how much effort he was putting into staying on drugs. For the first time, he saw just how much work it was taking to stay homeless, addicted, and ruined. And then he thought, "What would happen if I took all this effort and this hustle and I just put it to good?"

Discover a *More Powerful You*

I brought Gerald into this conversation with you because if he can do it, you certainly can. There's some area of your life where you are working way too hard and not getting what you want. You are fighting to hold onto something that just doesn't work anymore. What is it?

Imagine if you put that same amount of effort into getting what you wanted. If you could stop thinking about the past and only direct your thoughts forward, what would you love to accomplish? Clean slate, no baggage, no history—just the bright, open future. What would you want to spend your life doing? Write it down.

Now be powerful: *Tell someone and ask for help.*

From that moment he resolved to get sober. It wasn't as hard as he feared it would be. He just focused on the minute-by-minute actions he had to take to stay clean and do good. He went to a shelter, he checked into a detox program, and he forced himself to adopt a bigger state of mind.

We all think that it will take too much work to change our lives. We are wrong. Staying stuck takes work. Being comfortable but unhappy takes work. Just like Gerald, you need to believe that getting what you want will be easier than holding onto what you have.

In many ways facing a major crisis makes changing easier than just feeling blah. When you have a crisis on your hands, you are forced to deal with it. There's nothing like scraping the bottom of the barrel to make you realize that you have to change your life. The moment you receive a foreclosure notice, or lose your job, or lose someone you love, a grenade drops on your life and blows everything up. The severity of the situation forces you to react. If

Stephanie caught Aaron cheating with someone it'd be easier to make a decision about working on or ending her marriage. If Brian got canned during one of the rounds of layoffs and was forced to deal, it'd be easier than torturing himself inside his mind every day on the commute. As terrible as they are in the moment, crises are powerful because they destroy your routines and force change upon you.

When there's no crisis and you are just stuck, it is much harder to force yourself to react. There's no emergency. That's why it is so easy to postpone action. Day in and day out you just do the same old thing. Gerald's situation is extreme compared to your life, but after being a drug addict for thirty-nine years it was all he knew. It felt as comfortable to him as your commute to work. Because it was all he knew, that's all he did, until he admitted that staying stuck took too much work, and that getting what he wanted might just be easier. Now he has a shot to change his life.

Discover a *More Powerful You*

IF your life feels like a routine, try to pull back and ask yourself why. Try wondering just a little bit about what you're doing. Wondering about things is a terrific little tool to switch out of automatic mode and connect more deeply to the world around you. For every person you pass today, wonder what kind of underwear he or she is wearing. For every car you see, wonder how much gasoline is in the tank. You'll feel yourself more present in your daily life and kill boredom

> if you give yourself something to look for as
> you are going about your day. Kids are always
> doing this—looking out for something to discover.
> Imagine what might happen if you spent your
> day wondering and looking for things that relate
> to what you desire to change or make happen.
> Become powerful: Try it.

To get unstuck, you need the ability to see opportunities sitting in front of you and seize them. Whether you see those options or not depends entirely on your mind-set. The problem with routines is that you miss the detour signs and the signals to change direction. Lisa is so caught up in all the reasons why she can't make her dream happen that she misses the fact that there's a natural food trade show in town this weekend. Michael is so busy writing legal briefs and working crazy hours that he is not even aware that there's an open-mic night at a small bar every Tuesday night just three miles from his house.

I've got a friend whose job is website usability. He makes sure it's easy for Web-challenged folks like me to buy a book on Amazon. He once explained to me that while testing websites he started noticing something very weird. It seems that as the Internet was growing more popular, and more people were getting used to surfing the Web, he was discovering a growing group of Internet users who could look at and see certain parts of a Web page, like those annoying banner advertisements at the top of most pages, but they were never actually noticing them. Eye-tracking systems proved that they would pause and actually stare for a few seconds at the target advertisement, but when these people were asked to find the Viagra ads on the page, they were totally stumped.

In a way, that's not such a remarkable discovery. We've all heard that we're exposed to thousands of advertisements every day, and I'm sure you can hardly recall a single one by day's end. But further investigation proved that "banner blindness," as it's called, totally depends on the mind-set of the website user.

It turns out that aimless browsers, who were just strolling through a website without any specific agenda, were significantly more likely to notice things like banner advertisements. In contrast, website users with a specific task, and a targeted mission, missed things that were placed literally in front of their noses. All those task-oriented people had shifted their thinking into a routine mode, and robbed themselves of the ability to notice what they saw.

Aimlessness opens your eyes. If the world looks too familiar, and your routines take the color out of your days, you need to break out of the mission mind-set. When you break out of your routines, you give yourself something to look forward to. You introduce the element of surprise back into your life.

Research has documented the positive effects of breaking out of routines, and opening your mind-set to new experiences. Brushing your teeth with a different hand or getting dressed with your eyes closed not only stimulates the growth of brain cells but it also heightens your awareness because your mind can't zone out like it normally does. Numerous studies show that people who are stressed out and stuck in a narrow routine literally can't see the bigger picture. On the other hand, when you lighten up on the routine mentality, you start to see things that you never noticed before. And each new discovery broadens and builds your options. You set yourself up for a change.

Imagine you're ordering your coffee for the thousandth time from the Dunkin' Donuts take-out window, when you suddenly notice that the dreadlocked hippie cashier is reading an old Tom Wolfe book. Instead of just taking your change and staring at her nose ring like she's a freak, you ask her if she likes it. "Yeah, it's fantastic!" she beams, but says nothing more, and you've made a little connection.

Later at work, instead of just walking past the book-swap shelf near the copier, you pause and sweep the titles. Lo and behold, there's another Tom Wolfe book sitting on the shelves, so you decide to grab it. When you get home, after dinner's over and the kids are in bed, you notice the book on the counter and decide to skip watching television for once. Four nights later, you still haven't turned on the television and you're halfway through the book. You actually start wondering about the similarities between Wall Street in the eighties and today. You decide to rent *Wall Street* for your kids and reignite the old tradition of Sunday family movie night.

On and on. Breaking out of a routine creates a "butterfly effect" in your life. You change one little thing about your day and it can set off an entire chain reaction. Every new element that you introduce into your life becomes a clue to help you create a new direction. Every new direction is a pivot point in your life and a lever against inertia. Breaking out of routine is not a brute-force exercise. You just need to wake up and notice. What if Aaron stopped leaving the toilet seat up just because he knows it means something to Stephanie? What if Stephanie decided to make Aaron's favorite dinner and force herself to be interested in his day or give him a smile or a peck on the cheek when he left in the morning? What if instead of texting orders—"Pick up Sally at soccer"—they texted something else— "Hey, just thinking about you. Hope you're having a good day"? What if they started slowly trying to reforge that connection that's been lost instead of pushing each other further away?

Just by paying attention to what's hidden inside your routines, you will change. Quit with the efficiency—it's great for machines, but overrated for people. Slow down your routines and take them apart. Discover your own "banner blindness." You will end up finding small, positive things in your everyday patterns and build on them. This is exactly the kind of broadening of your daily life that leads to change. You will start to notice more around you and find more to look forward to. Imagine how different your day might look if you made a point of doing something uncharacteristic and creative. What's wrong with brushing your teeth with the opposite hand, taking a different drive home, using a different color pen? Imagine if you set about this change with a sense of humor, pulling back for a second and observing how odd all your ingrained habits really are. Imagine how different your life would look if you broke from your routine for a moment and admitted that your life could be so much more than it is.

CHAPTER FOUR

How to Outsmart Your Brain

One day I watched a yoga instructor come to my son's school and try to teach the kids a few poses. I had actually just finished a yoga class earlier that morning, so it was funny to watch all these little five-year-olds doing the same poses that I'd seen a bunch of adults struggle through only forty minutes earlier.

When the instructor showed the kids how to do "tree pose"—a tricky balancing pose that involves standing on one foot, while the other foot rests on your calf, and your hands are in a prayer position—I saw something remarkable. Most adults get the pose pretty quickly, but maintain a kind of tight-lipped, clenched-butt focused concentration in order to stay balanced for longer than a few seconds. The kids, on the other hand, couldn't wait to fall down experimenting with balance. Tumbling from tree pose was the whole point for them!

Just picture it. All those sweaty grown-ups cling to their center of gravity with a rigid grip, trembling muscles locked in a desperate bid to keep from falling down. Most of the time they don't fall down, but they strangle any sense of play from the exercise. They're like contestants watching the clock to see how long they can hold their breath. For adults it is about getting it right.

That's the problem with so many adults, we're all focused on getting it perfect, instead of trying. What ever happened to good enough? Why do we need to make the right decision every time? When we're constantly worried about making the right choice, we become paralyzed. That's why it takes something radical from you to act when you feel uncertain. You are pitting yourself directly against your own inflated expectations.

The kids, meanwhile, are running a whole series of miniexperiments with the gravity at work in the balancing act. They arrive in the pose, and as they start to lose their equilibrium, they'll quickly start waving their arms to regain it. They don't mind losing their balance a little, because they get to tumble down, and that's fun. In addition, they couldn't care less about the "embarrassment" of falling out of the pose, and they're happy to flap around—"wh . . . wh . . . whoah"—and draw attention to their so-called struggle. If you do the same thing as an adult, you feel like you are failing the class. They call yoga a "practice," but we tend to take all the practice and fun right out of it.

These kids are hard at work. They are exploring. Why aren't the adults? The biggest thing missing from your life is growth and exploration. You weren't always this tense and serious. You wouldn't think twice about scrambling up a tree, feeding meat loaf to the dog, busting out a dance move, or trying to make everyone laugh. What happened to you? Life silenced you. When you acted on impulse, life pushed you back in line. At some point, you learned that standing on your chair meant sitting alone in your room. Eating broccoli was a requirement *or else.* Don't talk so loud, you can't wear that, you must do your homework, that TV show's not appropriate, turn down your music, act your age, don't talk back, get off the computer, clean your room.

An implicit threat lurked behind your introduction to the rules of life. When you broke the rules, your parents used the predictable fear of punishment to activate your caution gene. It's cold but true. Gently tweaking kids' fears is pretty much the only way to get them to listen. Most parenting can be reduced to a simple bargain with your kids: Follow the rules, and you don't have to feel scared.

School reinforces the lessons and expands the bargain to include social rules. The basics are the same as at home: No running in the halls. Sit on your carpet square. Raise your hand. Stand in line. Wait your turn. But now there's the threat of getting kicked out of the pack. Kids in a group start monitoring one another. After getting the answer wrong only a handful of times, you quickly learn not to raise your hand when doubtful, unless you want to get teased later. If you want to be picked for kickball during recess, you need to make sure people don't think you're weird. Slowly, your instinct to take a risk, to raise your hand, to take a guess, to try something different from the herd became quieter and quieter.

By the time you graduated from high school, your life as an adult had begun. You kept your most important thoughts to yourself, your mastery of your own attention allowed you to ignore even those things that really interested you, and you'd learned a self-reliance that kept you from reaching out to others. The little explorer had evolved into a very different person and your DNA and your brain locked you into a rigid adult. It put too tight a grip on your life.

Now you may think I'm exaggerating. But consider the image of all those yoga folks hanging on for dear life. When you're hanging onto something and trying to be perfect at all costs, you crush any room for a more creative understanding of what's going on. You may not be able to see any options other than working long days, commuting twelve hours a week, and collapsing at night. But the truth is there are always a lot more options than you think.

You make the mistake of reducing your options every day. To preserve a sense of yourself as smart, you decide not to risk opening your mouth at a meeting. To keep the peace with your boss, you don't summarize the improvements you've made at work and request a raise. To maintain a friendship that's going stale, you avoid that tough conversation. You tell yourself that all of those things are fine, because you don't dare put anything on the line. You don't want to lose your balance, so you stick with a safe routine.

Change means risk. The status quo is a known quantity. Maybe you feel like your life is too fragile; you can't afford to break anything, so you hold on and protect what you've got. Doing nothing feels like the best bet from all angles.

That might make sense if you were a robot, and all you knew was routine. But there's a lot more going on in your brain. Your imagination is designed to come up with game-changer ideas for a reason. Your imagination is designed to push you in new directions and help you grow. You need to honor your own creativity and inventiveness by delivering change through action. Why would you torture yourself with all these ideas about losing weight, joining a rock band, finding your calling, falling in love, or starting a business if it was not somehow incumbent on you to live out your dreams?

It's Time for You to Be Bigger Than Your Brain

Your life is waiting to expand into something so much larger, and the only thing holding you back is your brain. You'll never feel like doing what you must do. Being powerful means being willing to be uncomfortable. You must be willing to fall. Whenever you find yourself overwhelmed with fear, clinging rigidly to what you know to avoid any kind of risk, that is a signal to take action. What you've done instead is listen to the infinite variety of persuasive arguments that your brain makes to convince you not to take action. When the time comes to lean toward what you want, you do nothing. To recognize these moments as a signal to act, to trust them and to do the opposite of what you "feel" like doing isn't easy. Learning to lean into things that make you uncomfortable takes practice. You are about to learn a method that will train you to build momentum in your life and become an expert at taking action.

If you've ever tried to lose weight or get in shape, you know exactly what it feels like to defy your feelings—it feels radical. You walk past a bakery and the smell of fresh croissants is wafting out the door. In that moment, you feel like having a croissant. You're annoyed as hell to be on a diet, so you start coming up with all kinds of reasons and rationalizations for breaking your diet. I exercised yesterday. I will skip lunch. I deserve it. I've been so good lately. To keep walking and ignore your feelings under those circumstances is the hardest thing to do. It feels wrong. As screwed up as it sounds, cheating on your diet feels easier—that's why you do it. And that's why your feelings can't be trusted!

If you want to find what's missing from your life you need to stop always doing what you feel like doing, and start doing the things that make you uncomfortable, the stuff you avoid, and the things that you think are hard. If you dedicated yourself to only doing the things you don't want to do, all day long, you would achieve everything you truly want. Make a mental list of things you avoid, postpone, and just don't want to deal with. If you attacked those today, your life would change.

You need to understand something that you've either forgotten, or no one ever taught you: What's "uncomfortable" is good. It only feels wrong at the start because you have an automatic bias toward the easy. You and your brain are creatures of habit, and you've simply taught yourself to take the comfortable route. But it's very possible to shift your style into one that commits to challenge. That's what it takes to get what you want. Not big scary leaps once a year. It takes small, but irritating moves every single day.

Trying to be happy when you aren't, or making do with what you have, or waiting for the right time to make your big move will not give you what you want. If you are addicted to your comfort zone, and only do what feels easy, you won't ever get what you want. People don't want to be on their deathbed, look back at their life, and regret all the things they didn't do. Nobody wants to say that his or her life was just "okay." But if you don't start doing what feels hard, that is exactly what will happen.

Choosing the path of least resistance is the core reason why your life isn't going anywhere. You're making hundreds of small decisions each day to stay exactly where you are. Not talking about improving your sex life is a decision. Not exploring new career opportunities is a decision. Skipping the gym every day this week is a decision. Not calling your brother and demanding that he come home to help care for your ailing mother is a decision.

Doing Nothing May Feel Easy, but It Makes You Unhappy

Our human behavior of taking the easy path actually makes no sense. By chasing easy pleasures, we lose happiness. Study after study has found that doing passive activities, such as surfing the Web in your pajamas or watching a marathon of *Mad Men* episodes, actually makes you unhappy compared to doing something active. Kids, for example, are much happier playing a sport instead of parking themselves in front of the television. In fact, they experience a higher level of enjoyment that has increased benefits to their mind and body, what researchers call "elevated excitement," when they play sports.

Despite that fact, when given the choice, kids are four times more likely to watch TV than head outside to kick the ball around. You are exactly the same. You love it once you are exercising, cleaning out your closets, or working on your résumé, but knowing that fact is rarely enough to push you off your ass to do it. Why would we spend four times more time doing something that has less than half the chance of making us feel good?

Psychologist Mihaly Csikszentmihalyi asked that very question in his seminal book *Finding Flow: The Psychology of Engagement with Everyday Life.* Csikszentmihalyi blames this tendency on "activation energy." This is the initial huge push of energy that's required to get a reaction—whether it is to get a stalled car to move forward or yourself out of a warm bed in the morning. Humans need that same huge push of energy to overcome resistance. If you don't get that huge push (like your mother turning off the TV and saying, "It's a beautiful day, get outside and go do something"), your brain will take you down the path of doing nothing every time.

What are you getting from doing nothing? Not much. In fact, after about thirty minutes of passive activity, you'll start to zone out completely. Psychologists call it "psychic entropy": It's that mental twilight zone where you completely check out when you do nothing. Your mind has basically stopped doing anything useful or productive. So why do you do it? Simple: You have trained yourself to hit the snooze button. If there's a way to avoid doing anything, you'll do it, even though it won't make you happy.

Discover a *More Powerful You*

THINK about it in terms of your own life. If you
continue to make the same easy choices you make
right now, what does your life look like in 2020?
Do you have the body you want? Do you have the
love life you desire? How's your job? Describe a
typical day in this future life in as much detail as
possible. Then ask yourself, is this the direction
I want my life to take?

Strategies to Outsmart Yourself

To become an expert at taking action you need strategies, because
there are too many things lined up against you. Willpower will not
work. It's not about waging a fierce battle with your instincts. You
need to learn to be smart about it. I'm going to teach you what it
takes to become an expert at ignoring your brain and taking action.
You'll have some simple exercises to try. You might want to dismiss
these exercises as corny, but chances are that when you give them
an earnest effort, you'll probably fail them. And then you'll have
to practice and practice and practice so that you can build up the
stamina, resolution, and momentum to really learn to push through
all your feelings, frustration, and fear to take action.

Yes, taking action is the way you start moving forward, but
to really get what you want and achieve your dreams, you need
strategies that take into account the native resistance you'll experience in your own mind. You'll need to follow strategies that let you

outsmart the feelings that are designed to slow you down. You need to help trick your brain into shutting up so the powerful you can take on a change.

The marshmallow test demonstrates what I mean by outsmarting your own brain. It's an experiment invented by Walter Mischel, a professor at Stanford University. Designed originally to test and observe children's ability to delay gratification, it attracted far more attention when a longitudinal analysis of its participants demonstrated that the marshmallow test could predict academic and professional success. A series of children were invited into an empty room, one at a time, and given the choice between eating a marshmallow now, or waiting to receive a second marshmallow when the experimenter returned later, but only if they didn't eat the first. For 70 percent of the kids, the marshmallow was gone within a few minutes. No shocker there; eating that sucker is the easy choice, resisting the urge is the hard action to take. But 30 percent of the five-year-old participants managed to avoid eating the marshmallow.

What really surprised the researchers was when they discovered that after following up with this same group of kids through school and adulthood, the ones who didn't eat the marshmallow right away consistently performed better in school and professionally as they grew up.

So what, right? At first this experiment seems like just another annoying vindication of all your schoolmates who did better than you. You just know that you would have popped that thing into your mouth before the experimenter left the room—and me, too. But a closer look at the details of the videotapes of these kids reveals something much more interesting. Careful observation showed that the kids who successfully avoided eating the marshmallow had simply mastered the art of distraction. It wasn't willpower or superior intelligence. They just used some simple tricks to outsmart the easy choice.

In their own five-year-old way, each of them demonstrated sophisticated strategies for denying the temptation and power of the marshmallow upon their thinking. The kids who tried to stare the marshmallow into submission just increased its overwhelming tastiness in their minds, and quickly gave in. But those who found ways to fidget, sing, play, or look away from the marshmallow managed to beat the clock.

The ability to master these sorts of techniques, and bring them into your repertoire, is called *metacognition*. It's basically the ability to beat your brain at its own game, by devising tricks that let you accomplish higher goals. There's nothing magical about them, and they are incredibly effective. Here's the proof: When experimenters tried a second round of marshmallow experiments with a new batch of kids, and taught all of them a simple cognitive trick, to pretend that the marshmallow was just a picture instead of a real treat, everyone's performance shot up dramatically—a far greater number of kids could wait for the second marshmallow.

The ability to outsmart your own shortcomings is what this book is all about. So many of us stare and obsess over our problems, and ignore what we really want, out of frustration and fear that we can't achieve it. In most cases, the only thing between you and the life you want is a small series of strategies that help you trick your brain into taking action. Right now your mind defaults to snooze. You always take the easiest route.

When you know that your feelings are working against you, success can only come if you defy your feelings and push through the unconscious resistance that is forming in your brain. When you are stuck, your feelings are running your life. Getting what you want means pushing through those emotional limits. Once you've decided on a goal, and confirmed that it makes sense in your life, you need to push through your inner obstacles, no matter what.

Emily is thirty years old and living in a small town outside Portland, Oregon, with her husband, Michael. She was a freshman and he was a senior when they met at college. They'd dated long-distance for the rest of her college career, and as soon as she graduated she moved to be with him, got married, and bought a house. Her first job out of college was working at her father-in-law's insurance firm. She threw herself into her job, worked long hours, learned everything she could, bought a car with her own money, took up mountain biking, opened up a 401k, and started feeling like she was actually an adult. A couple of years later she got up the nerve and made the jump to do her own thing. She bought a kit at a sales seminar and launched a network marketing business selling custom vitamins. She also bought a no-money-down real estate investing guide and started finding rental properties.

But after two years she was tired of badgering her friends about vitamins, so the network marketing business fizzled. The real estate market collapsed and her rental properties were barely cash-flow positive. Once again, her father-in-law helped her out with an introduction and she joined Century 21 as a commercial real-estate broker.

Most days she feels like a failure at work, and her home life is even worse. Her marriage is terrible—they've got nothing in common except two kids and a home. She badly wants out, but she owes her job to her father-in-law and has no clue how she'd raise two kids alone. So she does nothing. She works on presenting a "perfect" outward appearance to the world, reads a lot of self-help books that she never really acts on, and quietly tells herself that being happy isn't that important anyway.

She can spin off a mile-long list of reasons why change is impossible. But the truth is that her feelings are lying to her. If she pushed through her resistance and spoke frankly with her husband and told him the truth—that she wanted to either fix the marriage or get out—it would change *everything*. They could begin to work together to rekindle their love, or they could both start to move on. Her kids would benefit far more from having parents who were actually happy. Since she hates her job anyway, it makes no sense for her to attach so much fear to the idea of losing it. Like those children trading two marshmallows later for one right away, Emily is sacrificing all the happiness life has to offer just to be more comfortable in the moment. Just like those children, Emily needs to learn how to outsmart her own feelings to get what she really wants.

Many of your feelings—which you've grown so used to listening to, and that have been your greatest guide through all sorts of experiences—need to be seen as an enemy when it comes to reaching your goals. Due to their bias, they are telling you the opposite of what you need to do. When you cross your feelings, it is physically unpleasant. When you push through your limits, you don't feel good—your heart races, your stomach churns with anxiety, your skin feels prickly with fear.

There is a way to take action, even in the face of these feelings. Just like stage fright, or cold feet, or any kind of jitters, you can push through them and get to the other side. The solution is to adopt a bigger mind-set by focusing on what you want and then pushing yourself to work toward it.

I know what you are saying to yourself. This all sounds good, but there's no burning issue needing to be fixed in your life. Maybe you like your spouse, you still have sex on a fairly frequent basis, your job pays the bills—the problem is that you just feel checked out. You feel blah as you commute to work. Blah about your body. Blah about your clothes. Blah about your future.

Blah is still bad. Blah means something is missing from life. Chances are that you have done a good job convincing yourself that even if your life is underwhelming, it's quite comfortable, so what's the problem?

The problem is that you've bought your own propaganda. You're actively trying to convince yourself that it's okay to feel disappointed with yourself on a regular basis. You need to stop that now. Your life can be amazing. You can have what you desire. Feeling blah means you are stuck on a track in life and you've checked out. There is a simple method to get off of the track you are on and feel excited, inspired, and alive again. And I'm going to teach it to you right now.

Part II: *The Method for Becoming Powerful and Getting What You Want*

The people who get on in this world are the people who get up and look for the circumstances they want, and, if they can't find them, make them.

—GEORGE BERNARD SHAW

CHAPTER FIVE

Step 1:

Face It, You Are Not Fine

To regain control over your life you must stop pretending that everything is fine. The first step is to face the fact that your life has not turned out as you had hoped. Your brain works hard to insulate you from this fact. When it comes to the areas of your life that are blah, bothering you, or broken your brain does three clever things: It convinces you that you are fine even though you feel blah; it keeps you so busy that you have no time to stop and think about what's truly bothering you; and it focuses your attention on the surface-level, easy stuff that you feel comfortable talking about so you can ignore what's broken.

Convincing yourself that you are fine is a great strategy for keeping yourself stuck.
►*Stop it.*

Think about it: If it's not *that* bad, then there's no need to fix it. Howard has convinced himself for years that since smoking hasn't killed him yet there's no point in quitting now. Ellen told herself she was just a mom right now and could focus on herself later. Kathy thought, "This is it. I'm in an unhappy marriage and I'm a cleaning lady. This is my life. It's fine."

That's what we all do in the areas of our life where we feel stuck. That flab on your stomach is fine. Your crushing workload at the office is fine. Having two martinis every night to take the edge off is fine. Hardly having sex, that's fine, too. It's all "fine."

Maybe if pushed you'd concede that saying it's fine is merely a little white lie. Something you say because that's what everyone says. Since everyone is saying it, what's the big deal?

The big deal is that admitting the truth has enormous impact on your life. Powerful people tell the truth. And your little white lie is a way of diminishing the gravity of the situation and suppressing your true feelings. You need to be honest with yourself. If you feel unhappy, or you feel that something could be better in your life, you need to address it. Your feelings will just keep trying to push it underground because it is the easiest choice.

It's important to recognize that inertia is a form of suffering—the inability to realize our dreams generates frustration and fatigue and inserts doubts into our lives. Don't diminish that fact. When you doubt yourself you suffer.

You're so busy running around, you don't have a second to stop and think about your life.
► *Slow down, right now.*

Ever wonder why so many people return from vacation having come to important realizations about their life? Or why so many people who do yoga end up making significant changes to their lifestyle and career? The reason is simple. There's nothing like a long walk on the beach, spending some time in the woods, or ninety minutes in a downward dog staring at your toes, to make you slow down long enough to actually think about your life, where it is headed, and what you want.

One of the reasons you are so busy and frantic with your day-to-day life is to avoid contemplating such things. Your brain knows that. It's why it won't let you slow down. The times that you have the chance to slow down and think, you probably fidget like crazy or distract yourself with texting, just so you don't have to sit quietly and think. Your brain does that to you because if you did take a moment to get present and honest with yourself, you'd want to find a way to change things—which is the last thing your brain wants.

You pick easy, surface-level problems to work on so you don't have to tackle the tough stuff.
► *Time to go deep.*

Problems that you feel safe talking about are not really problems in my book. If you have some level of confidence that you may actually be able to fix these issues, they're more like annoyances. They are the fly that's bugging you, but you don't bother to get up and find a magazine to swat it. Every single day on my radio show, at least half of the callers are calling in about "fake" problems.

Sarah called into my show because she wanted help getting her boyfriend to be more considerate in the morning. Apparently he wakes up early and thrashes around the apartment and wakes her up. Sarah feels like he doesn't care about her feelings—it's all about him.

Dig a little deeper and Sarah starts describing a lot of controlling and inconsiderate behavior. Dig even further and Sarah confesses that Andrew is the third in a series of controlling relationships. The last controlling boyfriend, Sal, worked with her at NBC. He was a lot older and had a big job at the network. She was with him for seven years. Sal's parents disapproved of Sarah, so eventually he gave in to his parents and broke Sarah's heart. She tried to stay at NBC but just couldn't face the idea of bumping into him every day. So when the relationship ended, she left her dream job as an assistant producer and ended her career in television at the same time.

Does she describe it that way? No. As she explained so casually, she took a break from television to figure her life out. Five years later, she's a bartender working in a private doctors' lounge at a large hospital in New York. She lives in a studio apartment with a guy ten years younger who can't even pay half the rent, and she wants to know how to make him quieter in the morning. The relationship isn't Sarah's problem. The problem Sarah won't face is that her life is going nowhere.

She wants to work in television. She wants to be in a relationship that will lead to marriage. The moment we start talking about the real issue, she breaks down in tears. The relationship problem was just a decoy. She kept herself busy talking about her boyfriend thrashing about the apartment because it was just distracting and "safe" enough to avoid having to talk about the big, painful issue underneath: Her life is facing the wrong direction and she doesn't know how to change it.

The Role That Shame Plays in All of This

Admitting to yourself—let alone to others—that you're stuck can feel monumentally difficult. And just like most secrets we keep, it comes down to feeling ashamed. We all hate to confront our imperfections. Once we begin facing the truth that we feel stuck, the natural conclusion is that we've done something wrong.

When you're stuck, you experience disappointment and frustration on a daily basis. Whether it's the humiliation of doing work that is beneath your intelligence level and your creativity; or having to lug around a body that's a walking indictment of your bad eating and exercise habits; or the sad burden of living with someone you love who over time has become little more than a roommate; or the lonely regret of knowing that you've squandered too many years without ever chasing your dreams and now that the kids are off to college you feel like your life is empty of purpose—all these things fill you with shame.

Now you might have developed a more sophisticated argument that pushes away any similarity to shame, but you're still probably participating in a one-person PR campaign to bury your feelings. I'm not saying that makes you a bad person. Under the circumstances, that kind of denial may be very appropriate. If you've got a big road to climb in order to get your life back on track, that PR campaign may be helping keep you functional. Feeling miserable all the time is not sustainable. And there's no way you can confront and solve all your problems at once.

But from my perspective, unless you are actively exposing and airing your frustration and disappointment to yourself or others, whether it's only one-problem-at-a-time or the my-whole-life-is-a-mess shebang, you are actively keeping yourself stuck. The reason is simple: A hidden problem never needs to be fixed, so you are never putting yourself in a place where you *must* take action.

I'm not going to deny that there are plenty of good arguments for keeping your problems to yourself. I just think that these arguments don't stand up against the benefits of taking action. After hearing a litany of excuses on my radio show and through my life coaching over the last fifteen years, I can reduce all those arguments to a few basic categories of reasoning and all of which are bogus! Let's walk through them together, in order to help you identify the ways that you are keeping yourself stuck by simply not admitting the truth.

**We deny how we feel because in our society,
you're not supposed to be unhappy.**

There are all sorts of explicit and unspoken reasons for this. We all
know about the relentless chorus of positive thinkers who claim that
just thinking happy thoughts will change your life. Like Calvinists,
they urge us to constantly scrutinize our thinking for any sign of negativity, so we can somehow rephrase and push them away. They are
wishful thinkers who believe that by transforming your thoughts, you
will magically transform your life. But I've always considered *doing
something* better than thinking about it, and I would hate to monitor
my thoughts like an air traffic controller for signs of unhappiness.

Leaving aside the so-called magnetic frequencies of our thoughts
and the supposedly harmful radiation that emanates from negative thoughts, I think a more plausible explanation for hiding your
unhappiness is that we sense it's a social liability. People like to hear
about your problems only to the degree that it makes them feel better. There are some people who like to hear about your problems
because it allows them to offer advice. But as soon as they realize
that their advice is either stubbornly resisted, not being followed, or
totally useless, they quickly lose interest in hearing about problems,
and usually find subtle ways to let you know.

Then there are some who like to listen to your problems either
because they're just charitable, or because it allows them to cher-
ish not having the same ones—I never know which. But even the
most respectful confidant likes to talk about a variety of subjects.
The problems that come from feeling stuck are, by definition, repetitive and boring, and they will seem fairly uninteresting to others, especially if you aren't doing anything about them. Unless you
are actively attacking your problems and impressing your friends
through your efforts to fix things, frequent conversations about feeling stuck can be a major social downer.

Either way, it's a sad fact that no one really likes to hear about people who are depressed or down, especially once they start to sense that it's a long-term thing. People love gossip, but they don't like depression. "That's what therapists are for," they'll urge you, once you've exhausted their patience or their ability to help.

That creates social pressure to put on a happy face and talk about all the things that are going well in your life. But even though it might not make you the world's most popular person in the short term, if you don't talk about what's wrong, you are not merely misleading others, you're also helping to mislead yourself. I'm not saying you need to send out weekly newsletters to everyone expressing how you feel, but it is essential to find some vehicle for confronting how you really feel. If you're lucky enough to have an ally you can trust, that's great. But a journal can be just as good.

A key point to remember is that while people don't like hearing about problems that aren't being solved, if you can take positive action, it is much easier to win allies to your cause. Most people won't want to listen to you constantly complain about being overweight or hating your job—but if you start exercising or looking for a new job, you will be surprised how eager people will be to hear about your personal journey and do their best to help you.

Sometimes shame is actually disguised as pride.
Just as keeping quiet about your problems is a form of denial, so is keeping a stiff upper lip about them. Deciding that "life is tough" and that you're going to slog your way through it is just another way of shutting down growth. Behind this apparently stoic decision is a hidden refusal to take on greater challenges. It's not being tough; it's being cowardly.

Maybe you get some kind of inner satisfaction from knowing that you're better than the situation in which you find yourself. Or maybe you feel as if you don't deserve to realize your dreams, and you've decided to live your life as some kind of perverse punishment. Maybe you're creating a Cinderella mythology for yourself, with the secret hope that a fairy godmother will rescue you. In all of these cases, the simple truth is that no one is coming to save you. There is no one who is going to jump into your life and radically change its direction. And while it's true that no one can stop you from trying to soldier through your life, you will be much better off if you focus your energy less on your existential stamina and your ability to endure an unfulfilling situation, and focus much more on discovering and striving for what makes you happy.

One of the most insidious tricks your brain will play is to convince you that staying stuck is somehow the "moral" thing to do. It does this by drawing false comparisons. So you think that since keeping your head down and putting on a happy face in an unsatisfying marriage is, from an ethical standpoint, better than having an affair, that means it's the right thing to do. Since providing for your kids' needs is ethically superior to abandoning them by running off to do whatever you feel, that means staying in a job you hate is the "right" thing to do. You can take pride in being stuck, because it's a sign that you are a moral person.

But these dichotomies are false. It's true that having an affair or bailing on your kids is wrong. But those are not the only courses of action. You can talk honestly with your spouse about how you feel and either work to fix your relationship or seek a divorce in an honest and ethical way. You can look for ways to provide for your kids while still pursuing your passions, by either finding a new job or pursuing your hobbies outside of work. It is entirely possible to get what you want without compromising your integrity or sense of ethics. Being miserable doesn't make you a better person, it just makes you miserable.

Shame is also about exposure.

Even without the social code of always needing to appear happy, we just feel ashamed to expose ourselves. We all know the clichéd (but all too common) reasons for wanting to hide the truth, like the embarrassment of describing a sexless marriage, the frustration of working a job beneath you, the isolation of fighting a health problem, or the secret binges behind your weight problem. But another major reason we don't like to admit we're stuck is that we expose our mistakes.

Most of us take a lot of pride in our ability to navigate a complicated world. Our ability to make smart decisions is a sign of our personal success. When you talk about how your life is not going the way you hoped, you are exposing the hidden truths about your own life choices to others, and perhaps even your motivations. You are revealing that there are zones of your life that are—heavens!—not going well.

For some people, it's not so much that they can't deal with imperfection, but that they're forced to confront the fact that they made some poor decisions. To be unhappy in your job can imply that you made bad choices. Maybe you chose money over quality of life, and that exposes part of your character. Maybe you took a job because you thought it sounded cool, and you were hoping some of it would rub off on you, which exposes your vanity. An unhappy marriage can imply that you fell in love for the wrong reasons, or there's something about your character that drives your spouse away.

Here's the thing. When you have a problem that you can't get past, and you feel stuck, there probably is some sort of character fault that's lurking behind it. But who the hell doesn't have a character fault? Whether you like it or not, your faults are probably already as obvious to your friends and family as a wart on your nose. You're probably the only one who either can't see them clearly, or simply can't get comfortable with the idea of your imperfections. So maybe you are a bit argumentative, or selfish, or greedy, or lazy. Big deal. If you are avoiding the admission because you feel it will reflect badly on your abilities or talents or character, you are just continuing the problem that keeps you stuck. Put yourself on the line, and you can start fixing your problems and getting what you want.

Sometimes you don't want to admit how stuck you feel because you'll have to confess what you truly want.

Confessing your true desires can be really traumatic for some people, for a variety of reasons. Sometimes because it's so completely out of character, or against the grain of your social circle, or just plain expensive, that you're going to take a lot of ribbing and flak. The announcement of a financial analyst who wants to give it all up and become a restaurant owner is not going to be handled lightly by family and friends. Equally, the housewife who wants to go back to school and earn a master of fine arts is going to put a huge strain on her family for a very speculative return on investment.

Admitting what you want can be tough because stating clearly and confidently what you want means confronting what might be a huge gulf between reality and fantasy. Sarah is trapped squarely in this form of shame. If she admits that she wants to get back into television it means having to reach out to people from her past life—something she ran away from. It means admitting that these last seven years she's parked herself at a rest stop in life and hasn't moved forward. And then there's the fact that she'd likely have to start at the bottom rung again.

The dreams that we harbor about how our life can be sometimes sound pretty far-fetched. You may feel as if your goal is so impossibly far away that you'd rather not talk about it. You feel that it sounds ridiculous to talk about something that might take years to achieve and will take a tremendous amount of work. If you're a lifetime smoker, and you've got this urge to run the Houston Marathon, some people are going to chuckle when you put it out there. If you're working as a receptionist, people are going to have doubts when you talk about your dream of becoming an electrician. If you've spent the last eleven years home with the kids, people might question your decision to go back to school. There are few things more painful than watching an involuntary smirk show up on the faces of close friends when we talk about something dear to us.

Getting over the feelings of shame about admitting what you want is a crucial step in connecting your ideas to action. You need to be aware of how potent a role shame plays in keeping you stuck, and you need to push through that shame and express your dreams to make them real. The idea may sound preposterous, especially to your own ears, but the expression of your goal to others becomes a clear line in the sand. Whether it's about appearances or reality, admitting that you want more is the first step toward change.

Facing the truth is tough stuff. No one wants to collapse on her bed and sob over the state of her life. It's so much easier to stay busy, think about something else, insist that it's fine, and wait for the day when your mind-set will magically change and altering your life will seem easy. But that day is not coming. You will never just wake up with the motivation and fortitude that you've been missing for years. Your brain does not work that way. The only choice you have is to force yourself to change whether you feel like it or not.

You're like a kid who never feels like putting down his Game Boy and coming to dinner. You just have to force yourself to do it. Because when you postpone the moment for action, your resistance wins. The first step to killing resistance and taking action is to tell the truth.

I'm going to introduce you to two women who have a whole lot of resistance to changing their life. Both are divorced and raising their kids as a single mom. But there's one big difference. See if you can guess who will change her life and who will stay stuck.

Two Portraits of Denial:
Kathleen and Nancy

Kathleen

After seventeen years of marriage, Kathleen's husband, Jack, cheated on her with the twenty-six-year-old tennis pro at their club. The divorce was ugly. He got remarried and distracted by a new life with twin boys and a young wife.

Kathleen tells herself that it's better that he's not around much, but in her heart she knows their three kids feel just as rejected as she does. She was replaced with a younger woman, and they were replaced with a set of twins. She tried the online dating thing, but the few men she "winked" at never winked back, and she lived in fear that anyone she might meet for coffee would turn out to be a psycho. Her friends at work set her up on a blind date, but the guy had such yellow teeth she couldn't stop staring at them. The effort that was required to date was just too demoralizing, so she deactivated her online dating account and gave up.

She tells her girlfriends that a vibrator is as good as a man with a lot less hassle. Now she looks out to the future and has decided that she will probably be single for the rest of her life. And that's okay. After what happened with Jack, deep down she assumes that all men cheat and she can't risk that heartache again. She's fine.

She tells herself that it's better this way. She likes her routine. Her house is exactly the way she wants it. She can do whatever she pleases, whenever she wants. There's nobody waking her up by snoring, no nasty smell in the bathroom, no one's mess to clean up. Life is simple when you are alone. So why screw up a good thing by trying to date again?

Nancy

Nancy is in the same boat: divorced and single with kids. And in many ways, worse off than Kathleen because she is older.

One night her best friend, Janice, takes her out to dinner. Janice likes to push Nancy, and considers her a bit of a "project." She's constantly badgering Nancy to join Curves and come work out with her. Of course, Nancy always has a million excuses. She claims that these next few years have to be all about her kids, because they're about to leave home, and she wants to send them off with a good start. Besides that, Nancy says, she's got a full-time job. Janice also tries to get Nancy to date, but Nancy won't have it. She tells Janice, "I'm done with men. I don't need one." The truth is that Nancy's marriage had been horrible, her husband was a serial cheater, and the thought of going through that kind of pain once more makes her nauseous.

Her husband was the only man she'd ever really known romantically, so she can't figure out how she would start dating. It seems like guys in their sixties only want arm-candy—women in their forties. And older guys just want someone to take care of them. At sixty-one, Nancy feels like she is off the market.

Nancy has a nice time at dinner, and gets a little tipsy after three glasses of red wine. Her kids are with their dad for the weekend, so when she arrives home the house is empty. She checks her voice mail. No calls. Without anyone else in the house, she can do whatever she wants. She strips off her clothes in the middle of the bedroom and for the first time in god knows how long, Nancy catches a glimpse of herself completely nude in the full-length mirror. She is horrified at what she sees.

She is not the twenty or thirty pounds overweight she had rationalized, but more like fifty or sixty pounds overweight. Her stomach reminds her of what she looked like when she was six months pregnant. Everywhere she looks she sees fat. She even has fat beneath her breasts. She hates this mirror because she always feels fat when she looks at the stupid thing. But tonight is different. She can't turn away, and she can't lie. She isn't "chubby." She has let herself go. She has a problem; she doesn't need a doctor to tell her that she is obese.

In just a couple of years, her kids will be out of the house and off to start their own lives. The thought terrifies her. She sits down on the edge of her bed. Tears fill her eyes. She tries to swallow them back as she does in church during her favorite hymns, but they spill down her cheeks and she sucks in the stale air of her bedroom.

Nancy has just admitted to herself that she is obese, and even worse, that she feels extremely lonely. The tough shell has cracked. This is the truth. She can't lie to Janice anymore. And she can't lie to herself. She doesn't want her life to be like this. It feels like an eternity before she calms down. She lays very still and stares at the ceiling. For the first time in years, her mind is empty. The resistance is gone. Perhaps that's why she had always stayed so busy—as long as she was moving she didn't have time to think about how miserable she is. For the first time in years, she knows exactly what she wants. She wants her life back. She wants a man. She wants to be in love. She wants to have sex again. She wants to stop pretending everything is fine.

As far as which woman ends up getting what she wants, you'd better put your money on Nancy. Kathleen is still telling herself she is fine. Lying is easier than taking action. She's just scared to death of getting hurt again, so she resists taking any chances. That's why she took herself off of the dating site. That's why she concocted the story about how being single is better. The truth is that she would love nothing more than to lose the weight, look fantastic, and fall in love again. Kathleen actually fantasizes about showing up at her son's graduation with a man who is wildly in love with her. Not only would it be wonderful to rub someone who is more successful, more handsome, and more everything in Jack's face, but even better would be the inner confidence boost she would feel. But until Kathleen faces the truth and has the painful moment of honesty that Nancy just had, she will stay stuck and single.

To kill your resistance you must face the truth. The truth is powerful. Life delivers blows. That's the way it works. There will be moments in your life when you will be filled with pain. But the path forward is not making the best of a bad situation—it's making the situation *better*. Coping is the easy way out. Kathleen needs to admit that things have really gotten that bad, and that if there's going to be a real change in her life, she needs to fight for it.

It was incredibly difficult for Nancy to admit to herself that she was obese and lonely, but she is now one step closer to getting what she wants, while Kathleen is still stuck. When something is missing in life, pretending that everything is fine doesn't make the feeling go away. Kathleen can busy her life with her three kids, gardening, service league meetings, dinners with friends. But in those quiet moments on her morning walk she can't deny the feeling that she wished someone was walking with her. Facing the truth about your life can be terrifying because once you do, the task of fixing it can seem so enormous that you won't know where to start.

That's the reason you don't want to face the truth. Your problem seems too big to fix. Anyone can admit that she needs to lose five pounds because it is easily accomplished. But seventy-five pounds—that's a whole other story. If you hate your job, you can easily look for the same job somewhere else, but trying to figure out what to do with your life—that's a tall order.

You resist solving big problems because you feel uncertain whether you can. Pretending your problems don't bother you is a clever trick. But underneath the surface, you are like Kathleen, who walks alone, or Sarah, who left her job in television, or Michael, who works long hours at the firm. Underneath the surface lies the truth, that you are disappointed—with yourself, your career, and how your life has turned out.

It took Nancy a long time to face the truth. Some people never do—their resistance wins and they just carry on and bury the disappointment. We're all secretly dissatisfied with some area of our lives. Our rote response to people who inquire how we're doing is, "I'm fine . . . everything is great . . ." But at some deep level there's a sense of a dream denied, a yearning suppressed. But the fact is, when you tell the truth about your life, you have the opportunity to change it.

When Nancy awakes to the empty house, she feels disgusted by herself and her body and the way she relies on her friends to provide her with a social life. At this moment facing the truth, Nancy decides that she will change everything. She knows what she wants. She needs to have a plan to lose the weight starting today. And she knows that once she begins feeling better about herself, then it will be time to start dating and find someone to spend her remaining years with. No matter how much money she has to spend on gyms, trainers, nutritionists, and so on, she has to do this for herself.

She picks up the phone and dials information to get the number of Janice's gym. It is 6:30 A.M., but she is now on a mission. "Good morning, this is Curves," the voice on the other end says.

"Hi, I just wanted to make sure that you were open. I am

coming down right now and joining the gym. I need help losing fifty pounds." Nancy has admitted it. She has gone public and told a perfect stranger over the phone that she needs help. And instead of burying herself under the covers and feeling weak, she has done something radical instead. She has felt the power of facing the truth. She has taken one step by admitting what she wants and calling the gym. She is one step closer to getting what she wants, and one step further away from the life she can no longer stand.

Audit Your Life

The easiest way to face the truth is to take an audit of where you are right now. Various experiments have proven that the fastest way for a person to stop feeling stressed out is to put his or her feelings into words. A recent study conducted by professor Matthew Lieberman at UCLA used brain scans to prove that when participants took the time to write down their negative emotions, simply verbalizing the feelings made their mood improve. Turns out that writing down how you feel and describing the negative emotion decreases the activity in your amygdala (the alarm center of the brain).

There's also an immediate improvement to your decision-making skills. In *Your Money and Your Brain,* Jason Zweig explained that your negative emotions tend to hijack your decision making and cause you to make really dumb decisions, especially with money. When people write down their negative feelings before they make financial decisions, they make better ones. Similarly, studies show that dieters who write down what they eat lose twice as much weight as dieters who rely just on their heads.

When you stay inside your head and ignore your discontent, you tend to forget details and make emotional decisions. When you hold onto the stress and negative thoughts in your head, they build on each other and grow into something larger. To date, your emotions have been dictating the action you take. That's why you chose the easy path—it *feels* right. Something as simple as writing down how you are truly feeling is where you must begin if you want to take action. That's exactly what you will do now: Take an audit of where you are in your life.

Your life is made up of these seven areas:

> **FAMILY**
>
> **LOVE AND SEX**
>
> **SPIRITUALITY**
>
> **CAREER/PURPOSE**
>
> **FRIENDS/COMMUNITY**
>
> **BODY/HEALTH**
>
> **MONEY**

1. On a scale of zero to ten, **rank your level of satisfaction** with each area of your life. Zero means total disaster, and ten means paradise.
2. Describe briefly why you ranked each area of your life the way you did. Do you feel blah and just kind of stuck when you think about this area of your life? Are you bored with this area? Could it be better, but for now it's fine? Is this an area of your life that feels broken?
3. Why are you not changing? Refer back to your earlier exercise about mind-set. Are you acting like a jerk or a chicken when you think about changing this part of your life? Have you thrown a wet blanket on the future? Are "what-ifs" stopping you?
4. What would make your level of satisfaction go up in each area of your life?

Don't get hung up on being exact. Just rank each area based on what your gut tells you. This exercise lets you do something we rarely allow ourselves to do—step off the treadmill and assess where we truly are in life. You can directly describe your life and all its moving parts. The questions are there to help you stop for a moment and clarify with yourself where you really and honestly are in life—much as you would if you were taking a long walk on the beach or staring at your toes on a yoga mat.

Next, I'd like you to think about these areas of your life individually. Answer these questions to help you really narrow in on what's bugging you most. Don't try to rush through the answer. Take your time and consider each area carefully. Answer each question fully and write down the reasons.

1. Which one of these areas is the best part of my life? Why?
2. Which area of my life am I the most proud of? Why? What would I need to do to make myself as proud of the other areas of my life?
3. Which area have I worked the hardest to change? Did my effort pay off?
4. Which area do I stress about the most? What do I stress and worry about exactly? Rank the level of stress from zero to ten.
5. Which area is the most important to you? Which one are you the most disappointed in?

Now that you've taken a moment to explore the seven major areas of your life, let's start addressing each one. Take a look at your notes. There are things that you want to change about your life. Perhaps in just one area, perhaps in all. There are things you could be doing to make yourself happier. But you just won't do them. Let's take some action:

Start by getting a separate sheet of paper for each area of your life. Then for each area, go through the following exercise:

1. Draw a line down the center of the page. On the left side of the paper write at the top: "What Bugs Me." In that column you will write down all the things that bother you about that area of your life. Things that you want to fix. Don't settle for fine anymore. You want more. When you look at your social life, tell the truth. You wish you had a closer circle of friends. You would love to feel more connected.

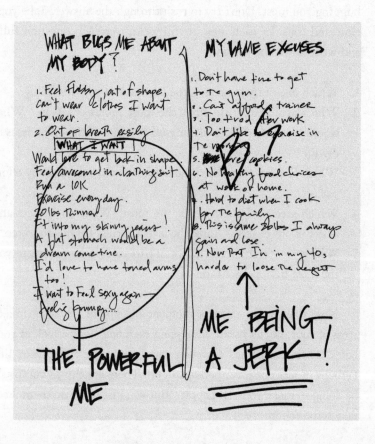

2. On the right side of the paper write at the top: "My Excuses." Underneath it write down all the reasons you feel that you can't change that area of your life or are afraid to try. There should be many reasons. *It's too late. I don't know how. I don't have the money. I'm afraid. I'm not qualified. I've tried this before.* Write them all down.

3. Now take a step back. What this simple little exercise does is draw out your excuses. Not only is your brain overloaded from the demand of modern life, it is fried with your excuses. You've jammed it full of so many reasons *not* to take action that it's no wonder you feel stuck. It cannot entertain any new ideas. As long as you attach more value to the right side of this paper than to the left, resistance wins. Now that you have written down the negative emotions, you are in a position to see them coming and ignore them.

4. Pull out a permanent marker and write THE CHICKEN AND THE JERK across all the things you wrote down under "My Excuses." Whenever these excuses come up and you feel yourself resisting action, your job is to be powerful and push through. The more you write with the marker, the better. Check out this example on page 126.

5. Hang up the paper above your desk or on your fridge (or put it on your bedside table—you want to see it every day) to make sure it stays top of mind. You are going to systematically hunt down and kill your excuses, so I want you to be familiar with the target. In the past, these excuses stopped you. Today, if you hear them coming to the surface, you will take aim and power right through.

Don't blow off the task of putting this list somewhere you can see it. Winifred Gallagher's book *Rapt: Attention and the Focused Life* explores a simple theory: Your life is the sum of what you focus on, therefore managing where you put your attention is the key to happiness and fulfillment. Gallagher argues that in the world of e-mails, cell phones, cable TV, and texts, we are totally overloaded because there are too many things demanding our attention. According to scientists, we remember only one of every hundred or so things that come across our mind. Like a cup that's filled with water to the brim, anything new that you pour on top will just spill over the edges and be lost.

This phenomenon is why you can receive an e-mail, think *I've got to reply to that,* but then get distracted and focus on something else almost immediately. It takes just one phone call, one text, one more e-mail, or a Twitter alert to pop on your screen and it's already slipped from your mind. That's why you need to put this somewhere where you'll review it daily or use this trick: Type it up and e-mail it to yourself every morning as a reminder.

Now that you understand the feelings and excuses you need to push *through,* the question becomes what are you pushing *toward,* exactly?

CHAPTER SIX

Step 2:

Admit What You Want

You've fessed up about what's wrong and identified the tricks your mind uses to keep you stuck. Now it's time to admit what you want.

Your deepest desires are the most important tools you have to help you push through resistance. It's time to use them. Your desire acts like a honing device. If you tune into it, it will point you in the direction you are meant to go. Admitting what you really want is the way you harness your desires and develop momentum.

This might sound obvious and simple, but it's not. To admit what you really want can be embarrassing. It can seem like a cliché, or sound patently impossible. The idea that you might not get what you want can be so terrifying that you avoid even admitting you want it. Or maybe you don't even know what you want—you just know you're not happy with what you have.

But as tempting as it might be to avoid admitting what you really want, you must. If you do, you will instantly give your life some direction, a beacon to keep in sight. You will feel less afraid, which will make it easier to avoid taking the easy choice. And in imagining your future, you will start to build it.

Admitting It Focuses Your Attention

Psychologists have done hundreds of studies around something called "inattentional blindness." It's the phenomenon that we often miss what is right in front of us unless we are completely focused on it. The most famous experiment involved a short YouTube video, in which about half a dozen guys perform Harlem Globetrotter–style tricks. Your job is to count how many times they pass the ball. After about twenty seconds and thirteen passes the screen goes black and a question appears: Did You See The Gorilla? You think, huh? The video rolls again in slow motion, and lo and behold, a dude in a gorilla costume is moonwalking across the background and you totally missed it. When researchers did this, 46 percent of people missed the gorilla.

I was one of them. I was so dumbfounded, I started the video right from the start and sure enough, now that I was looking for him, his presence was obvious. You miss an enormous number of opportunities to change your life on a daily basis because you are not focused on what you want. You are focused on your problems and maintaining the illusion that you are fine. Until you face the truth about your life and start focusing on opportunities to take action, you will continue to miss the gorilla moonwalking in the background.

Admitting it gives you something to look forward to and to push toward. And because you are focused on what you want, your brain gives its full energy to achieving that goal.

I was late to work, and probably shouldn't have even been driving. The snow had started at 5 A.M. and had been coming down heavily for more than an hour. I had decided to try and beat the morning commute, and it was still dark outside. I came to the stop sign near the state highway, and my wheels just locked up. I slid across both lanes of the deserted highway road, and onto the opposite shoulder. In full denial of the situation, I quickly swung into reverse gear and tried to back onto the road, but my wheels were spinning. I tried to rev it a few more times, and rock the car with the gas and brake, but nothing worked. Eventually I had to get out of the car and assess the situation. I needed to understand whether I needed a shovel, a push, traction, or a tow.

The same is true with life. When you first realize you are stuck, you try to keep going and you end up spinning. You try a few tricks, but getting unstuck isn't so easy, and you go nowhere. Eventually, as with a car, you have to assess the situation so you can figure out what you are dealing with. And what's your first reaction when you realize you are stuck? Annoyance, frustration, maybe a sense of dread and helplessness. A constellation of worries. Nothing that's going to help you move forward.

Focusing your mind on what you desire will kill the worry. It will give your brain a specific job, which will help you focus on solving your problems instead of being overwhelmed by them. The more you can crystallize and clearly imagine what you desire, the better the chance that your mind can help you get it. Desire keeps your momentum high and helps you stay focused so you get unstuck.

Plus, by admitting what you want you can harness the power in your brain to help you achieve it. Researchers have uncovered a skill in your mind called "outcome simulation." It's one of the most powerful weapons you have to kill resistance and find your momentum.

In study after study, researchers have proven that when you direct your mind to think about an outcome you desire, you eventually start to believe that it is going to happen.

You can make this technique more effective by intensifying it with "process simulation." That's when you think about not merely what you desire, but you also visualize all the small little mundane actions you would be taking to get you what you desire.

Am I saying that if you visualize yourself running down the bike path outside, in your new Under Armour shorts, feeling fit and healthy while listening to some thumping dance song on your iPod, that you'll get your butt out of your chair and do it? Absolutely! And the more detailed an image you can cook up, the faster your resistance will disappear. The technique is even more effective if you take it a step further and shift from seeing yourself in the scene, to actually being in the scene. Visualize the road and the scenery unfolding in front of you as you are running and you will have just gone from seeing the image of yourself in Under Armour shorts to inserting yourself mentally into the simulation in the first person and feeling as if you are running. Seeing it from that perspective is the most powerful method to motivate you.

I used to be terrified of flying, and for good reason. I was once on a plane that hit an air pocket, dropped a few hundred feet, and lost pressure in the cabin. The oxygen masks dropped, the A/C started condensing, causing water to pour out of the ceiling panels, and the captains told us to brace for an emergency landing in the Atlantic. It was the longest ten minutes of my life. I thought for sure that I was going to die in a plane crash. Obviously, I didn't. We made an emergency landing in Puerto Rico and everything worked out fine. Except for the fact that after that experience, I was terrified to fly.

From the moment I started to think about a trip, I would avoid buying tickets until the last minute possible. The night before my flight, I would live in fear that this would be my last supper with my husband and children. All I saw in my future was death by airplane crash. I'd suffer a panic attack from the moment I woke up until the moment I landed. I was so afraid of flying, I couldn't watch the show *Lost,* because the images of that crash in the first episode only made me torture myself more.

While I was on the plane, I had all these little tricks that I tried to use to calm myself down. As soon as the approved electronic devices announcement came on, that was one checkmark in my brain that we would be okay. The beverage cart service was another. The seat belt sign being turned off meant I was home free. And then it occurred to me. If I simply thought about all the things I was going to be doing once I landed, that would help me direct my mind. I thought about deplaning. I imagined myself greeting my parents at the gate. I thought about the meal I would eat and pictured myself at the table. The more images I could see of me on my trip, the more the resistance disappeared. After all, if I was eating dinner with my parents later that night, obviously the plane landed safely. "Process simulation," focusing on images of myself getting what (or in this case where) I wanted, killed my fear of flying.

Once you admit what you want, you can use "process simulation" to accelerate your results.

You Are Crafting Narratives
That Keep You Stuck

Admitting what you truly want can be extremely tough for some people. That's because most of us tell ourselves that we can't have what we want or don't deserve it. There are few things that human beings find more compelling than a story. We use stories not just for

Discover a *More Powerful You*

WHAT'S something you've been wanting to do?
Try process simulation to make action easier. Close
your eyes and picture yourself doing that activity:
Are you opening up your new retail store; are you
starring in a TV show; are you speaking Spanish;
are you getting married?

Now, take it up a notch. Visualize in the first
person. Don't picture yourself sitting at your
computer writing your novel—visualize what you
would actually see: your hands typing and the
computer screen. Don't picture the big mansion as
you drive by it, visualize what it looks like as you
turn the key, unlock the front door, and walk into
the foyer.

entertainment, but to make sense of the world and our place in it.
We turn our lives into narratives, and cast ourselves as the heroes.
This might not sound problematic, but consider that when you turn
yourself into a hero and build a fairy tale about your place in the
world, it allows you to reinterpret everything wrong with your life in
a way that makes it seem fine, admirable, or outside of your control.

You might hate that you're overweight, but you tell yourself a story
in which it isn't your fault—you can't go to the gym and diet because
you need to keep the house clean and have dinner ready on time for
the kids, so you're too busy. Your lack of fitness isn't a character flaw;
it's a sign of how noble and self-sacrificing you are. Or maybe you hate
your job but can't find the courage to strike out for something new.

But you tell yourself a story about how losing this job would mean losing your house, put your kids out on the street, and leave you broke and penniless. Your willingness to waste day after day doing something you hate isn't a personal flaw, it's a sign of how prudent and cautious you are, and of being a good parent. You might be in a loveless marriage, but you tell yourself that you're fine with it, that only selfish people would ever get divorced and that you could never be so selfish. Your lack of genuine passion makes you a better person.

When you tell yourself a fairy tale and turn yourself into a hero, you make staying stuck seem like the right thing to do. You deny your true desires, because you convince yourself that not getting what you want makes you a good person, or that getting what you want is impossible so only stupid people would waste time thinking about it.

These stories can take a variety of forms. Maybe you don't really know what you want, but instead of taking that as a cue to explore new experiences and broaden your horizons, you just convince yourself that you don't want anything at all. Maybe you're scared of what other people will think, but instead of finding the courage to shrug off the judgments of others, you tell yourself that their opinions are more important than yours, or that they know more than you do about your own life. Maybe you simply delay and give in to fear, but you tell yourself that you're really just being cautious.

Perhaps there are logical reasons why you can't get what you want right away, but instead of thinking of how to overcome those reasons, you convince yourself that they are "just the way it is" and you can't do anything to change them. This kind of storytelling is called "obstacle thinking," and the key sign you've fallen prey to it is that you stop seeing barriers to success as problems to be solved, and start seeing them as incontrovertible facts of life.

One of the most popular stories is the "either/or" story. This is when you fall into the trap of believing that you need to sequence your life. You tell yourself that getting what you want is so monumental that you can't possibly do it without upending your life. When you're locked into this kind of narrative, you frame your life as a bowl filled to the rim—add anything to it, and it will overflow and you'll be left with a mess. You probably view your days as completely booked with one thing or another. So when an opportunity comes along that you hadn't expected, your default response becomes "no," because it doesn't jive with your objectives in an obvious way.

But being powerful is a lot more than checking things off your list and sticking to a rigidly regimented life plan. It's about expanding your horizons, constantly moving outside your comfort zone, and experiencing new things. When you hear about a new opportunity, the first word out of your mouth should be yes. Not "let me think about it" (aka no), or "I think that might work" (aka no), or "I'd really like to" (aka no).

When you set yourself in motion, you're going to be moving through the world at a higher velocity, and you're going to be crossing more opportunities, more often, and with more frequency. If you're living in an either/or world, you're deliberately putting on the brakes, and depriving yourself of opportunities that could actually be changing your life for the better. You need to have a "both/and" attitude. Why can't you be a manager at the Gap and an actor? Why can't you be a lawyer and a bass player? Why can't you be a mom and invent a product for QVC?

The either/or narrative always frames new ideas in terms of massive, inseparable amounts of work. So learning a new skill doesn't start with taking a single night's class—you have to sign up for a full master's program. But that would mean giving up your job, which is a complete impossibility, so the whole idea's off the table. By framing the decision as something that requires a total and radical change, you make it unrealistic. But the truth is that your life is a lot more elastic than you're pretending. There is always room for more action in your life. The either/or narrative is a lie.

Another popular narrative is the "I'll lose everything" story. Every great novel has high-stakes drama, and you love to bring drama to your own life as well. You do this by tying every dream you have to losing everything you've got. You'll start telling yourself that you can't afford your dreams, that chasing them will mean losing your house, your kids having to drop out of school, and going bankrupt. You go from idea to the "I'll lose everything" story so fast, you don't even have time to let your desire really sink in. Your personal fairy tale transforms your dream from something wonderful you could achieve with a little effort, into a disaster waiting to happen.

You can't admit what you truly desire when you are telling a story. As comforting as your narrative might be, you must break out of it, and deal with reality as it actually is. Here's how you do it. First, consider the seven major areas of your life:

FAMILY

LOVE AND SEX

SPIRITUALITY

CAREER/PURPOSE

FRIENDS/COMMUNITY

BODY/HEALTH

MONEY

Now, in every area of your life, ask yourself: what do I truly desire? Examine your own mind for a moment. Forget about money, bills, time, and whether or not you think you can do it. If time and money were not an issue, and you knew you could pull it off without embarrassing yourself—what do you want to change about your life? What is one thing that you would really love to have happen in your life? Is it a new job? A new relationship? More balance in life? A rock star body? A big break? To get pregnant? It can be anything at all. Take a minute to think of it. As soon as it enters your mind, write it down and be ready for the negative stories to kick in. As soon as you spit it out, your mind will consider all the obstacles, excuses, and reasons that this is a bad idea. You'll tell yourself the "I'll lose everything" story, or the "either/or" story, or the "I'm not that sort of person" story. Your brain will try to get you to reject the idea, or to shrink it down to something so meager it barely excites you. You might have written "I want a new and wonderful career," and your brain will try to turn that into "I want a moderate raise." You might have wanted to become a gorgeous person who looks like a model, and your brain will try to turn that into "I want to lose ten pounds."

But if you want to build momentum and become powerful, you must expand your thinking at this stage, not shrink it. There will be time to shrink it later. As you write what you want, fight back the urge to shrink the thing you desire. If you want to lose weight, tell the truth about how much. If you want to lose seventy pounds, fight off the urge to say fifty. It might seem as if shrinking your dreams makes them easier or more manageable, but the truth is that when you shrink your dreams you kill them. The smaller version is not what you desire. It's a lie. The little thing is not what you want, the big one is. If you're overweight, the idea of being slightly less overweight won't motivate you. Being fit and healthy and beautiful, on the other hand, absolutely will.

Double-check your work. Whatever you wrote down has probably been shrunk in some way. To really nail it, it has to pass three tests.

►Test #1: Is It Embarrassing?

What you wrote down must be embarrassing to admit. When you dream about something cool and big enough to inspire you, it's going to be quite far from where you are right now in life. That gap is embarrassing, which is part of why admitting what you want is so hard. If the thought of telling someone you know about this desire makes you feel nervous and embarrassed, it's a good one. Expand your idea and make it bigger and bolder until you would be nervous to tell someone.

►Test #2: Is It Selfish and a Little Crass?

Every last one of us is motivated by our selfish desires. Once you admit what you desire, go a little deeper and figure out why you want it. The reason can't be all goody-goody. The reason must be selfish and crass. Even if you say "I want to help people," the reason you want to help other people is selfish. You feel good when you do it. That's why you want to do it. And that's cool—you *should* want to feel good. But "helping people" *sounds* so much better, that's why you say it. But what sounds good isn't going to be what really motivates you. What will motivate you is getting exactly what you selfishly desire.

Why does it need to be so selfish? You aren't going to get up, push through all the bullshit, and take action until you have a good reason. Being nice, being liked, being the biggest goody-goody you can be—those are not good reasons, and they aren't going to motivate you to get off your butt and change.

Take Joseph in Indiana, for example, who called into my radio show looking for help. He is twenty-four years old and packed on over fifty pounds during college. I asked him how he had gained so much weight. He explained to me that it was the unstructured nature of his days at college that made him gain the weight. I said, "Joseph, that's a lie—it wasn't the lack of structure, you went crazy on the meal plan and frat parties and you let go, didn't you."

"Yes, ma'am."

"Okay, stop lying about the reason you gained weight. This is your fault, you got lazy."

"Yes, that's true."

Next I asked Joseph why he wanted to lose the weight. And again, I got another lie for an answer.

"Ma'am, I want to lose weight because I give blood every month and I noticed my cholesterol has been rising steadily."

Now my memory is still fresh enough to remember that there isn't a twenty-four-year-old man on the planet who cares about his cholesterol. Twenty-four-year-old men care about one thing—having sex. "Joseph, let's level with one another—this has nothing to do with your health, does it?"

"Ma'am?"

"Joseph, you hate your body, don't you? When you look in the mirror, you see a beer belly and a set of man boobs and you hate it, correct?"

He laughed. "Yes."

"How's that faring with the ladies? Not so good, huh?"

"No, ma'am."

No one wants to admit that he hates some aspect of his life, so you come up with all these fruity reasons that you want to change. Something that sounds good. Joseph couldn't tell me the truth that he hated how fat, flabby, and unattractive he had become. Saying his cholesterol needed lowering sounds better. But it's not true. He doesn't give a hoot about cholesterol. Cholesterol is not why he wants to change. The real reason he wants to lose weight is selfish and crass. He wanted to lose weight because he wanted to look good. He wanted women to want him. He wanted to be better in bed. He wanted a girlfriend.

No wonder he never shed a single pound. By concocting some nonsense story about rising cholesterol as the reason he wanted to lose weight, he'd robbed his dreams of any power they might have to motivate him. If, on the other hand, he had said to himself, "I'm a fat and lazy slob and if I don't get this lard off, there's no way I'm hooking up this summer," that's a powerful reason to exercise. The truth is motivating. That's why you need to tell the truth about what you hate about your life and the crass and selfish reasons you want to change it. Sex, money, winning, recognition, and just having fun are all wonderful motivators. You don't need to broadcast it to others, but you must embrace your selfish desires internally to take action and motivate yourself.

Many times people shy away from their selfish desires, because they equate "selfish" with immoral. But this is a false equivalency. Immorality means hurting other people. But you can go after what you want without hurting anyone else. Joseph isn't doing anything wrong by trying to improve his sex life. If you're worried that acting selfishly means you're doing something wrong, just ask yourself if anything you're doing is dishonest, hurtful, or otherwise at odds with your sense of right and wrong. If the answer is no, then you have no reason to feel guilty about trying to realize your selfish desires. Being a good person doesn't mean being a martyr.

►Test #3: Is It Specific and Detailed?

Unless you spell this out with such detail that it seems like a blueprint for what you want and when you want it, it will not work. You are not allowed to write down something vague like: "I want to make more money," "I want to be happier," or "I want to be healthier." You must force yourself to pick something very specific to do.

When I asked Joseph what he wanted he said "to be healthier."

That's not a goal. It's too vague and it's not that inspiring. For a goal to work, you must bring specificity to it and it must be something that's beyond where you are right now. "Be healthier" is a lame goal. If Joseph were to lose one pound, technically he'd be healthier. If Joseph were to knock a couple of points off that cholesterol reading, he'd be healthier. For this to be useful, Joseph has to make his dream specific. "I want to find those six-pack abs, wear a size 34 pant, prove all those bastards at the fraternity that called me 'fat ass' wrong, and hook up by labor day." Now *that's* a goal worth taking radical action on.

Shaping your goals into something that is truthful and specific is essential. So take another look at what you wrote down and start filling in details. If you're dreaming of finding a man—describe exactly what kind of man. Is he funny, charming, sexy, successful? Great. Does he like Maroon 5, enjoy traveling, and race triathlons? Even better. The more specific you make this, the more powerfully you will be motivated. And don't worry, you aren't narrowing the field—you are increasing your own enthusiasm and motivation to get out there. If you want a better job, write down what you'd like to do all day, how much you'd like to make, what perks you want. "A better job" isn't half as good a motivator as "a job making at least a hundred thousand dollars a year, with an assistant to handle my busywork, good vacation time, and work that keeps me traveling and meeting new people." When you get what you want, it might not align 100 percent with every specific thing you detailed, but that's okay. This isn't a binding contract. It's a motivational tool, rocket fuel to boost you into action. And the stronger you can make that rocket fuel, the better.

Now look over what you've written. Is it embarrassing, selfish, and 100 percent specific? Good. *That* is what you want. And if you follow my advice, that is what you'll get.

What If I Don't Know What I Want?

If you are sitting there thinking *I don't know what I want,* then one of two things is true about you:

1. You actually do know what you want. You have just done a darn good job of convincing yourself it's not possible. Every time you creep near what you want, you quickly retreat and start saying to yourself, "But what if . . ."
2. You truly don't know.

If you know what you want but you don't really feel comfortable with it, then you have no choice. Admit it.

Emily (the Century 21 Realtor in Portland, Oregon), for example, is terrified of her marriage ending. Is she happy? No. Does she love her husband, Michael? "I love him, I'm not in love with him." Does she want to be a single mom? No. Does she want to face the disappointment of her parents and her in-laws and her husband? No. The easy choice is to stay married. The easy choice for most of us is to focus on work and trying to be happier there. The even easier choice would be to distract yourself and have an affair, like Brian (the mortgage guy) is contemplating with Molly. Another easy choice is to bargain to postpone your life: I'll wait until my two-year-old leaves for college and then we'll separate. But the truth is Emily wants one thing—a happy marriage. And the fact is, she is miserable.

Emily needs to stop focusing on the solution (which she thinks is ending the marriage) and start focusing on what she desires. This doesn't mean thinking things such as "Michael and I used to do all kinds of stuff together but we got married so young." When you focus on your desire, do not raise the past ("we used to do all kinds of stuff together"), insert reasons why you can't have it ("we got married so young"), or worry about how it affects your current life or the people in it. Simply focus on what you desire.

If Emily is honest with herself about what she wants, her thoughts would look something like this: "It'd be so nice to be with someone who I have things in common with. We'd be true partners getting stuff done around the house, making money. We laugh a lot and do things together like hiking, cooking dinner, travel, and having friends over. He makes an effort. He surprises me once in a while. He sends me texts to just tell me that I'm beautiful. I'd like to feel connected to him and to work together on our shared goals."

Emily knows what she wants. She just couldn't state it until now. She needs to write this all out and sit down with Michael and explain in detail what she wants from their marriage. Then the ball is in Michael's court. If he wants the same things, they can work together on taking action to evolve their marriage. If they don't want the same things, then Michael and Emily can make that choice together as well.

But what if you aren't like Emily, burying your true desires beneath a mountain of fear-driven excuses? What if you really just have absolutely no clue what you want? You might be surprised, but in that situation the solution is even simpler. Just pick *anything* that you are curious about or that pops into your mind, and then go explore it. It actually doesn't matter what you pick, as long as it's something new. The act of exploring something cool or new to you will automatically broaden your life and lift your attitude. Your problem is that you keep waiting to be struck with some kind of life-altering, lightning-bolt, incredibly inspiring idea—but if you aren't doing anything new, there's nothing in your life that is going to inspire you. You have to force yourself to move and expand first,

Discover a *More Powerful You*

WHEN you identify what you desire (rather than fixating on what's broken and the obstacles to fixing it) you can now start to take action. Start by writing about a day in the life you imagine. What time would you get up? What is the morning routine like? Write about what happens during the day. Detail what it would be like when you arrive home from work. Write out what the evening is like. Put as much of it into the first person and describe what you see, feel, smell, and taste as you move through the day. By focusing on what you want, instead of concentrating on what you have, you will be giving yourself a map to guide you in a new direction. Great, now be powerful: Spend one day pretending your life is as you imagined.

and then the idea will hit you. Sitting around thinking isn't going to take you anywhere. You need to get out into the world and do something new and exciting and big. What you need is action, not thought. So stop thinking and just pick.

I sat in my office struggling over words to describe how to explain this idea to you, and my ten-year-old wandered into the room and let out one of those classic melodramatic sighs that she's learned from television.

"Mom, I'm bored."

"So go clean your room."

"No, really. Nothing ever happens around here. It's the same old, same old."

Discover a *More Powerful You*

DO not underestimate the power of a whim. A whim is not a left-field impulse that comes out of nowhere to steer you into danger. A whim is only possible because it's been building in the back of your mind for a long time. You've been mulling it over casually but never acted because your resistance was in the way. Over time, it doesn't feel so risky anymore, so you can "on a whim" do it. Malcolm Gladwell had been thinking about growing his hair long and crazy like he used to wear it as a teenager. And then he decided to do it "on a whim." As Gladwell said about his hair, "Immediately, in very small but significant ways, my life changed." One of the most significant ways long hair impacted Malcolm was an incident when three police officers jumped out of a van because his long and wild hair resembled that of a suspect they were chasing. As Gladwell puts it, "That episode on the street got me thinking about the weird power of first impressions" and that led to his bestselling book *Blink*. Whims are a window into your desire and they change your life in small but significant ways. When you feel one brewing, it's because it has been building for a while. If you had the time in this moment to act on a whim, what would you do? Would you contact someone you admire? Would you go to a yoga class or attend a seminar on entrepreneurship? Would you plan a trip? Cool. Be powerful: Go act on it. Quickly.

"What do you want to happen?" I said.

"Anything! Nothing different ever happens. It's so boring living in this town."

"You want someone to get kidnapped or something?"

"No. I dunno. It'd be nice to have some big fair. Something to look forward to."

"Go clean your room and then you can start looking forward to dinner."

It's never a great idea to let your ten-year-old realize she's smarter than you. She rolled her eyes and huffed away, while I sat dumbstruck. After three hours of trying to put an idea into words, my daughter had nailed it cold. Getting unstuck isn't about sitting around the house, trying to will yourself out of boredom. It's about giving yourself something to look forward to. It doesn't have to be some rigorously plotted ten-point plan for changing your life. It just needs to be something fun that will shake up your day, give you something fun to anticipate, and change your perspective. That's why all you need to do is pick something new to explore, and when you are busy, you won't feel so stuck.

You've done such a bang-up job getting your life into a predictable routine that there's nothing big on the horizon that you are anticipating. Having something to look forward to elevates your mood. When you have nothing to look forward to, you feel stuck. You can hear it in the voice of every one of the callers to my radio show. It's the thread that unites all their stories. Whether it's an unsuccessful marriage, a runaway career, a dream gone AWOL, or a stay-at-home mom wondering if this is it, each of them was missing the sense that something cool is happening in their lives. They're stuck on the treadmill. But any new thing they decide to explore will get them off that treadmill and shift that feeling.

That's why you can just pick anything that strikes you to explore and pursue.

A little while later I walked downstairs to get a glass of water and saw my daughter lying on the carpet of the playroom, laying down tracks on her brother's train set. She was totally engaged and smiling as she played with her little brother. Hardly the brooding, bored preteen she was just thirty minutes ago. Now if I had suggested that she go downstairs and hang with her five-year-old brother, she would have dismissed the idea out of hand. When you get out there and just do something, instead of obsessing over the "right" thing to do, you'll be surprised at how quickly you'll find something you enjoy.

If you don't know what you want, all you need is to pick something to relieve your boredom. Something that makes you feel like you are doing something. It doesn't have to create world peace, you don't need to make a million dollars with it—you just need to relieve yourself of feeling so bored with your life. Thinking won't relieve boredom. Only action will work. My daughter could have gone outside and thrown the ball for the dog, worked on a bracelet-weaving project, made cookies, written in her journal. Anything she picked would have gotten her to stop thinking about how stuck she felt and would have focused her mind on some activity instead. You need to do the same thing with your life. Stop thinking there's a right thing to pick. It doesn't *matter* what you pick.

Some people are lucky enough to know exactly what they want. You don't, so you will have to take action until you bump into it. Everything you pick to explore will give you data that you will react to and that will help you shape the always-evolving answer to what you want.

I can't stress this point enough. Even if you pick something to take action on and explore, and a month later you realize it isn't what you are interested in, that's fine. First of all, you won't be bored anymore because you'll be focused on exploring something you are curious about. Second, everything you learned during that month you will use to help you figure out what to pick next. Getting out there and exploring is the only way to figure out what this next chapter will be.

I used to be a lawyer. In 1999, I remember sitting at my desk in a high-rise office building dying a slow death of boredom. I hated working in a law firm but had a mortgage to pay. I could not "think" my way to what I wanted to do with my life. I didn't know how to get unstuck at the time, so I made all the classic mistakes. I thought about my mortgage and focused on what I could do with my law degree. Never in a million years would I have thought about the idea of being a life coach or radio and TV host, or writing a book. It wasn't even on my internal radar screen. All I knew is that I just didn't want to be doing what I was doing.

The one thing I did right was focusing on action. And for me, that meant talking to other people about something I was curious about—the dot-com boom that was happening in Boston at the time. I also toyed with the idea of opening up a bakery, something I'd thought about off and on since I was a little girl. I didn't know which impulse, if any, was the right one. But that didn't matter. I just knew I didn't want to be doing what I was doing, and that's all I needed to know to get started.

I asked the owner of a local bakery if I could work behind the counter for free for a couple of days. I wanted to shadow that morning baker and learn the ropes. It was a very valuable experience. When I tried out my dream by working in a bakery, I realized I didn't want to get up at 5 A.M. and bake. I didn't want to wash that many pans. I didn't want to have to scrub down the equipment and the counters, fill the milk and half-and-half pitchers and napkin

Discover a *More Powerful You*

WHAT is boredom exactly? To answer the question, researchers at the University of Michigan, led by Daniel Weissman, put volunteers into an MRI and asked them to do something that was mind-numbingly mundane—identify letters on a screen for an entire hour. And then they studied what the brain did as the poor volunteer was trapped in the MRI, probably questioning his decision to sign up for this experiment. They noticed that areas of the brain closely related to self-control, vision, and language processing seemed to stop almost all activity. When the brain stopped, inattention and boredom were triggered. Boredom occurs when a part of your brain switches off. The question is, what can you do to switch it back on? The answer, figure out something you would look forward to in your future and start to chip away at it. Taking action is the only way to flip the switch back on. According to Stephen Vodanovich at the University of West Florida, who has been studying boredom for over twenty years, if you find yourself chronically bored, it is because you cannot figure out what the right thing to do next is, so your life feels mundane. The irony here is that there is no "right" thing to do next—any shift in focus will relieve your boredom. If you are standing in line at the deli counter, bored and zoning out, all it takes is for your number to be called to snap out of it. You can simulate that by simply finding something right now to focus on, instead of zoning out. To reverse the flow of boredom, just call your own number. Scan the room you are in and see if there is anything at all that reminds you of something you want or that seems like it could be fun. It doesn't have to fit in with some grand life plan, or be the

flash of inspiration that instantly gives your life
purpose. It just has to seem like it could be an
exciting way to break up the monotony. Now go
do something about it.

dispensers every fifteen minutes, and wait on people all day. I didn't
want to smell like morning glory muffins and dish soap.

What I realized by just picking this idea and taking action is
that I wanted the kind of life where I could have a "bakery experience," but I didn't want to own one. Basically, I wanted to live in a
town that had a great local bakery. I wanted to have the flexibility
in my schedule to be able to swing by in the mornings and afford
a latte on a daily basis. And I wanted the sense of community that
comes along with walking into a bakery in the morning and having someone say, "Mornin', Mel, want the regular?" Because of what
I learned, I could cross "retail" and "bakery" off of my list. And
I could make a mental note that finding a lifestyle that gave me
the flexibility to enjoy small moments and little daily luxuries was
important to me. With that, I turned my attention back to exploring the dot-com scene. Did that suddenly mean that it was the right
answer after all? Not necessarily. But even if it didn't turn out to be
what I wanted, by exploring new things I'd expand my horizons,
and I'd be one step closer to figuring out what I really did want.

So right now pick one thing that you are interested in or curious about. It could be something you've thought of doing since you
were a kid, another person's life that you are secretly jealous of, or
just something you happened across one day while channel surfing
or reading a magazine that you thought looked fun. Now go explore
it. Whether or not it's the right thing for you is irrelevant; action
will kill your boredom and take you one step closer to discovering
what you want.

CHAPTER SEVEN

Step 3:

Go Public with What You Want

Until now, you've been working on these steps toward changing your life and getting unstuck by yourself. It is important work, but it's been inside a bubble. Now it's time to take your first step into the outside world—you will open your mouth and speak. The reason for going public is simple: Communicating is one of the most productive forms of action you can take. When you share your ideas, or ask for someone's help, you're learning subtle new skills about yourself and others every time. And at the same time, you're advancing your own personal agenda and taking concrete steps toward your goals. Ask anyone who went through law school, and he or she will tell you that you can't really learn how to truly think on your feet without sparring with a partner. Preparedness and memorization counts, but there's something else you learn when you rely on your verbal skills and perform a mock trial.

That's because plain old thinking relies on well-worn, overused circuitry. School has gotten us all proficient at memorizing and juggling ideas in our minds. Thinking is not hard. It's when we're forced to socialize an idea, convey meaning in a persuasive manner, and juggle facts and rhetoric that our brains are really challenged and we discover what we're capable of. It's a skill that must be acquired, and studies have shown that thinking on your feet lights up completely different parts of your brain. According to researchers at the University of Southern California, the sort of quick-witted social thinking that comes from activities such as bridge or enjoying brisk conversations with friends also has a huge impact on fighting dementia in old age. Speaking, defending, and explaining ideas offers a much tougher mental workout. Simply put, talking about what you want will help you build the mental strength you need in order to get it. And just as important, by talking about your goals, you help make them real. When you sit around and think, "I should lose weight," you haven't really changed anything. But when you announce to the world that, "I am going to lose weight," you enlist the outside world in holding you to your commitment.

There are three simple reasons why you cannot skip over this step:

1. You can't get anything done in life without the help of other people.
2. Other people accelerate your pace and broaden your ideas.
3. Your relationship with people is the most important aspect of your life.

You Need People to Get Stuff Done

Almost everything you do in life requires the help of other people, including going to the bathroom indoors. That toilet you sat on this morning—someone halfway around the world made it. And then someone at the distribution center loaded it onto a plane or a truck. A trucker drove it to a warehouse, where a bunch of people moved it around a distribution center, where another trucker took it to the store where you bought it. Then another person logged it into an inventory tracking system and then someone put it on the shelf for sale. You might have had someone help you get it down and put it into your car, but not without a cashier ringing you up first. Then you had a plumber install it.

Yes it's true, even something as private as using the facilities required other people's help. The simple truth is that you can't jump-start any idea without the help of other people. I learned that one the hard way. We had been watching one of my kids play an early evening soccer match—an away game. After a trip to the Porta Potti, we piled into the car. I got everyone settled and buckled my little guy into his car seat. It was starting to get dark. Then I went to start the car . . . and nothing happened. Silence. Uh-oh.

I wasn't prepared. We were an hour from home. I called my husband but he didn't answer. So I did what anyone would do in my situation: I leaned my head on the top of the steering wheel and told my kids to shut up while I contemplated how bad this was.

"Wait," I thought. "I'm not unprepared at all! I have jumper cables!" I bounded out of the car, out into the dark parking lot, and opened the trunk. There they were. I was all set. Perfect! I had jumper cables.

I looked around the parking lot. A few cars, but no people. I chucked the cables back inside the trunk and slammed it closed. I learned something very valuable then: You can't give yourself a jump start. My kids and I eventually found someone to help, but even if we'd used AAA, we'd still have been receiving help from others.

When people say they want to jump-start their life or career, it sounds like something they do themselves. But how do you really jump-start something? You ask for help. To accomplish anything, you must ask for help. You may have all kinds of tools, big plans, and great ideas at your disposal, but you still need someone to help you. You can't do it alone.

Other People Accelerate Your Pace and Build on Your Ideas

Connecting with other people is part of your genetic wiring. When you "click" with someone or make a positive connection with a stranger, your body releases oxytocin. Studies show that oxytocin in your bloodstream immediately reduces anxiety and improves your brain processing powers. You experience this effect in your own life countless times, anytime you make a positive connection with another person.

Let's say you go to a dinner party and are seated next to Mike, whom you've never met. As you start to talk, you realize that your best friend from college grew up in the same town as Mike. He didn't know your best friend directly, but he played football with her older brother. From there you realize you've both just finished reading the same book, and on and on the rapport grows.

When you click with someone you feel an instant rush. You realize you have something in common, you start speaking faster and smiling more without even realizing it. That's the oxytocin kicking into your bloodstream. Even with a perfect stranger, if you smile enough and hold eye contact in a friendly way, you'll feel a genuine bond with the person you are interacting with, even if he is simply bagging your groceries. I love those moments when you feel the zap of energy from making a connection with someone. If you do it right, you can almost feel the oxytocin hit.

There's an exercise that every motivational speaker breaks out at some point. Whether you are at a yoga retreat, a sales meeting, or a leadership workshop for your church choir, some version of this basic exercise is coming your way. The instructions are simple. First, pair off with someone. Then stare into each other's eyes. One of you should smile as genuinely and widely as you can while looking deeply into the eyes of the person. The other person should try to return the look and look right back into the eyes of the first person. But, and here's the catch, the second person is not allowed to smile, smirk, or react in any way to the first person's smile. Just remain still and expressionless. Within ten seconds, the same thing always happens. Almost everyone bursts into laughter. Why? Simple, scientists have discovered cells in your brain that are called "mirror neurons" that can copy the feelings, actions, and even sensations that another person feels. If someone else is smiling, you just can't help it, you have to smile, too.

You feel this urge to mimic in lots of ways. Yawning and laughter are the most well known. But you also flinch when your friend cuts her hand slicing cantaloupe. You can practically feel the knife scalping the tip of your own finger right off. That's your mirror neurons duplicating the sensations inside your own head. So what, right? Well, if you can't help but mirror the emotions, physical sensations, and actions of people around you, then you can use that to your advantage to help propel yourself forward and learn how to build an instant rapport with the people around you. This is part of why surrounding yourself with positive, motivated people is so important, because you'll be naturally inclined to mirror their emotions and behaviors.

I'm an eye-contact addict. It's a secret power source that you can use to boost yourself all day long. Why they don't teach this in school is beyond me. Don't take lightly the value of making friendly

Discover a *More Powerful You*

LAUREN Zander introduced me to this eye-contact game, and I want you to try it! When you walk around today, make and hold eye contact with four people you've never spoken to before—and if you're really game, make them complete strangers. There should be someone of the opposite sex in there, too. But either way, he or she must be someone with whom you've never exchanged more than a hello. Here's how you do it. As you pick your target, stare into his eyes. The game starts when he looks back into yours. Hold your eye contact and break into a genuine smile. Whether it's a big toothy one or not is up to you. But look friendly and real—and don't worry, you'll feel so goofy you won't be able to help but smile. And then, hold your eye contact and count to four. One. Two. Three. Four. You'll notice a couple of things. You'll feel a surge of energy from the exchange as he picks up on your gaze. And if he smiles back, your mirror neurons will make you fire off an even bigger smile. A connection is truly infectious. If you ever feel yourself in need of a momentum boost, use this technique to jump-start yourself off the energy of some stranger!

contact with people you see every day. Those little hits of oxytocin can mean the difference between feeling blah and feeling like you can do anything. And just as minor connections with strangers can give you a boost, so can deeper connections with people you know but haven't opened up to. It can do a world of good to open up a little to someone at work or at the gym whom you get along with.

Emotional Support Is
Essential to Your Health

IN the 1980s, there were heartbreaking accounts of children left in institutional isolation inside orphanages in some of the poorest nations overseas. Romania got the brunt of the scrutiny, and without going into the grim details, studies found that children in these orphanages lacking physical contact and emotional engagement had vastly different hormone levels than their parent-raised peers. Their cortisol levels, a hormone connected to stress, were profoundly higher even into their adult years.

Isolation in adulthood has a negative affect on you as well. University of Chicago psychologist John Cacioppo analyzed the data on thirty years' worth of research in his book *Loneliness* to prove that as an adult, the lack of meaningful connections can lead to depression, higher blood pressure, and be as deadly as some diseases. When you have the social support of friends, family, neighbors, and colleagues, on the other hand, the positive impacts are innumerable, from improving your chances of surviving cancer, to reducing stress by knowing that you can vent with someone about a toxic work environment. Positive connections are your best defense against a world that wants to stress you out.

By sharing more of your personality, you create room for a better connection and you make the world a little bit friendlier for yourself.

Another way that people help you build on your ideas is because they ground you in the idea. Research has proven again and again how important your personal relationships are in making you feel connected to your place in the world. Trying to change can be a very lonely process. You tend to isolate and work on yourself quietly. When you involve other people, it makes your goal that much more real, not some fantasy you are watching in your mind.

As Ann Bigelow, a professor who studies parent and infant development at St. Francis Xavier University, points out, babies only know that they are "active agents" in the world because they can see that their actions affect others. When we mirror a baby's coos and smiles, it's not to help teach them that adults are goofy idiots. We're helping them recognize that their feelings and actions have a direct impact on their environment. They learn that we're all living on the same planet, and that other people care about those feelings and actions. A connection with others brings you reactions, feedback, and ideas to push you forward in a way that no force you could summon on your own ever could. The more you share yourself with others around you and talk about your plans and goals, and the more that other people are helping you figure out how to accomplish it, the better developed your idea will become and the more you'll feel inspired to take action.

Relationships Are the Most Important Factor in a Fulfilled life

Positive connections with other people create depth and meaning in your life. One of my closest friends (and next-door neighbors) while growing up is now getting his Ph.D. in psychology at Northwestern. He's been working for the past four years with a famous study commonly referred to as the Harvard Men study. He explained it to me one night over beers that in the late 1930s, researchers began tracking 250 men's lives at Harvard University, and they've been following them ever since. Almost half of the men in the study, well into their eighties now, are still alive. Researchers like my friend Mike have been poring over this rich and extensive data to spot trends in everything from marriage status, to jobs, to geography, to financial security in order to discover what makes people live the happiest and fullest lives. Mike had been traveling the United States interviewing the remaining survivors of the study as the basis for a thesis and a book he's working on. He shared with me several insights about what creates meaning in someone's life.

His conclusions were best summed up by George Vaillant, the psychologist who directed the study for more than forty years, in an article in *The Atlantic* last year marking his retirement. Vaillant said that relationships proved to be one of the most fruitful areas of study. When men were forty-seven, the quality of their relationships predicted late-life adjustment better than any other variable. When asked what he had learned most from studying every detail of over 250 men's lives over a period of fifty years, Vaillant responded, "The only thing that really matters in life are your relationships to other people."

It turns out that the types of conversations you are having with those people in your life matter, too. Dr. Matthias Mehl from the University of Arizona tracked eighty college students with electronic devices and found that the more meaningful the conversations students were having, the deeper the connections they formed. It's not surprising to learn that the type of conversations you hold will have a direct effect on the depth of your bonds with others. It makes sense. If you only talk about the weather with someone, you probably don't consider him very important. But if your good friend came to you because he had a deep desire to go back to school for his nursing degree and wanted your help, wouldn't you feel flattered and closer to that friend? Of course you would. When you speak to your friends about the things that really matter, it strengthens your relationship to them and to your own happiness.

Of course, there is nothing more personal or important than your deepest desires, so by telling others about them, you will strengthen your personal bonds in a way that will immeasurably improve your life and happiness. In short, talking about what you want isn't just a tool for helping you find happiness, it is one of the best ways to make yourself happier and more fulfilled immediately.

Discover a *More Powerful You*

TODAY only have conversations that cut beneath the surface. No conversations about sports, weather, or the news. If someone says he or she is fine, dig a little deeper. Ask questions. Be interested in how these deeper conversations affect your mood. Ask the cashier how his day is going. I told a cashier at Trader Joe's who was scowling, "You don't look like you're having a good day." He replied, "It's horrible." I asked why and he explained that he had just quit smoking. We spoke for a bit about why he chose to quit (turns out, his daughter was going through chemo for breast cancer and it was for her). From that day on, whenever I see him at Trader Joe's we catch up about his daughter's health and his life as a nonsmoker. Be powerful: I dare you to try to unearth something surprising from a cashier today. It's one of my favorite things to do when I'm out running errands. If you do manage to get someone to admit that he's not fine, you'll be shocked at how good it makes you and him feel to know that someone cares.

Making Your Goals Public

Reaching out to others can be very hard. We all want to change in secret, in the privacy of our own cocoon, before we emerge completely transformed. Nobody wants to expose those ugly, awkward moments of true change to the world. It's a bit like navigating puberty. When you're in elementary school, you feel fine. And eventually when you're grown up, you become comfortable with yourself again. But when you're an awkward teenager with braces and acne, you'd rather lock yourself in your room then come out to face the world. Change feels embarrassing. And things get even tougher when you need to ask others for help, because it means burdening other people with your issues. It's much easier to keep most things to yourself.

Our culture emphasizes keeping up appearances at all costs. But being powerful requires honest contact and communication. The people around you can help you get what you want. But if you keep your dreams, goals, and disappointments to yourself, that will never happen. You have to let your voice hit the airwaves. You *have* to go public.

The paralysis and hesitation you feel when you think about

sharing your mind with others is just like any other form of resistance—it's a signal to act. The fact that it scares you is a sign that it can bring about real change in your life. The truth is that by itself, even reading this book is not going to magically change your life. Which is why I'm not going to let you get away with simply reading it. Before we're done, you're going to have to take action.

Right now you are probably trying to backslide from the whole "go public" thing. You might even be feeling a little betrayed. You figured out what you want, you put it through the test, made it as embarrassing, selfish, and specific as possible. And now I'm asking you to go tell someone about it? It probably seems horrifying.

But I'm not telling you to go public just to be mean. I'm telling you to go public because no matter how scary it might seem, it is the *only* way that you are going to change your life and get what you want. You need to push through these feelings and be bigger than those fears.

But what if your goal wasn't really your deepest desire, what if you just didn't know what to write, so you just wrote down some stand-in idea because I said you had to? Well, too bad. That doesn't let you off the hook. You've still got to get out there. You're saying to yourself, "Go public? But I'm not even sure I want to do photography. I just picked it because I was told to." It doesn't matter. Go get advice about photography and ask your friends for their insight on what they think you *should* be doing if not taking photos. The conversations will broaden and expand your options and get you out of your head.

Now, open up your contact list, pick the first three names that jump out at you, and call them. Tell them that you have been feeling stuck lately and wanted their advice on an idea you are exploring, a goal you have, or something you desire to make a reality. And try to get excited. Even if you're shaking in your boots, fake some enthusiasm. The more excited you sound, the more excited they will be to help you (mirror neurons at work again).

These people want to help you, and talking about your desires will help you make them materialize. You have permission to ask your friends, colleagues, neighbors, ex-classmates for help. If there is one thing that people love, it is to give advice and feel like they are helping someone out. So pick up the phone and make the call. If they are somewhere near you, set up a meeting. If they live too far away, just talk to them on the phone. Tell them, "This is what I am thinking about doing . . ." Then describe your desire. Ask the following questions and any others that come to mind:

1. If you were me, what specific things would you be doing to get started/learn more/etc.?
2. Do you have any books you'd recommend I read?
3. Do you know anyone who could give me some more advice/ counsel?

Finally, follow up with them a week later.

This last step is critical. After you take their advice and speak with their contacts, you need to follow up. There are a few reasons why. First, because it makes them feel great and builds a stronger bond with them. They are then further invested in your goals and desires. And if you learned anything from their advice and tell them about it, your friends may have additional ideas to help broaden and build even further. Second, by checking back in with them, you give yourself a bigger incentive to actually take their advice to heart. If someone tells you to read a certain book, and you're never going to speak to him or her again, you might not do it. But if you know you'll be speaking again shortly, then you'll feel pressured to get off your butt and go read that book.

It is as simple as it sounds. The worst that can happen is that someone doesn't have much to offer you and you've wasted five minutes on a phone call. Big deal. It only feels hard because you hate asking for help, looking vulnerable, and feeling like a burden. That's your brain putting a wet blanket on this idea. But once you're talking to your friends about your life and goals, you'll realize that far from feeling painful, it feels great. So ignore your brain—it's wrong. Be powerful and make the call.

Maybe the advice you'll get from your friends will stink. Maybe it's no different from what you've already cooked up yourself. Advice isn't the point. Moving forward is the point, and moving forward can't happen in secret. You need to bring everyone in your world along with you.

Once you have your conversations with your friends, you don't have to stop there. You can ask these questions of anyone you happen to bump into. People love to give advice. Have you ever had someone tell you to buzz off when you asked for directions? Of course not. Everyone loves to feel like he is in the know and of service to someone else. You can also use perfect strangers to help you stay on track when you feel yourself getting weak or scared. I've reached for the hand of my seatmate on a flight that had some pretty alarming turbulence. One of the best ways to go public is to ask other people to "make sure" you don't or do something. Check out how Mary did this at a luncheon awhile back.

Mary was a seasoned dieter. She'd yo-yoed up and down the scale for her entire adult life. She was also no stranger to leaning on other people. She contracted lymphoma in her late thirties and took three years off from her job at a firm on Wall Street. During those years battling her disease, she had an army of friends helping her. When she was fighting cancer she let her friends and family help her get through those three difficult years. She hadn't been embarrassed by cancer so the help was easy to take back then, but she was very embarrassed to be so heavy. Unlike cancer, she saw it as something that she should be able to control herself. Asking for help was embarrassing, so she dieted in secret. When I met her, she said that she was going to a women's business luncheon and was worried about the dessert table.

I told her that willpower wouldn't work. She had to use tricks to outsmart herself. She had no problem ordering the salad, but the moment when everyone at the table got up and went for dessert worried her. She could envision herself sitting there alone and feeling the shame and pressure. She was convinced that she did not have the willpower to avoid the table. Either way she was screwed. She was contemplating leaving the event right after the lunch entrée to avoid the whole scene altogether.

"There's another option, Mary."

"What?"

"Use the other people at your table to help you stick to your diet," I said.

"How do you suggest I do that?"

"Tell them you're committed to losing 120 pounds and you are not allowed anywhere near that dessert table and it's their job to keep you from it."

"No way. Then they'll know that I'm trying to lose weight," she replied.

"Mary, you need to lose 120 pounds. I don't think they'll be surprised that you're on a diet."

She went to the event. And after the lunch was cleared, she told the other women that she needed their help. She explained that she was dieting, had zero willpower in situations like this, and under no circumstance should they let her get up and get a dessert.

A funny thing happened. The other nine women around the table gasped with delight. "Me, too!" "I shouldn't go to the table either!" They were all on secret diets. It's not that surprising, considering that almost forty-five million Americans are on a diet right now.

If Mary hadn't gone public with her request for help, they probably all would have silently cheated on their diets. But by going public, Mary got the support she needed and realized something even more valuable—everyone is trying to change something, we're all just too afraid to admit it.

Going Public to People
You Love Isn't Easy

Telling a spouse or a parent about your big idea can be a heck of a lot harder than telling a colleague, a friend, or a mentor. That's because your family members have known you for a very long time and have locked in certain opinions about what you can and cannot do, and what you should and shouldn't do. They may be the ones who are least likely to believe you can change based on past history. Or maybe they are going to be directly invested in making sure you *don't* change. If they're directly affected by any big decisions that you make, they can't give you truly objective counsel.

Maybe following your dream means telling your husband that you're not going to be available on certain nights, or that you're not going to be helping out as much for a few months. Or it could mean telling your wife that you're no longer happy in your marriage, and that certain things have to change if you're going to make it as a couple. Or simply admitting to your friends that you feel like a loser.

Doug had spent the last nine years toiling away at jobs he hated. He wanted his own business, but he could just never figure out what type of business or how to pay for his life while he launched it. His wife, Sally, was very risk averse. Her response to his list of ideas was always the same, "Sounds great, but until you write a business plan, get funding, and can afford to quit your job, there's no way you can do it." Doug could never push past the stage of just thinking about it. He was too embarrassed that he was stuck, so he didn't tell anyone. He decided he would wait until he had a rock-solid idea and a business plan written proving it before he would reach out to his network. Of course, in practice this just meant he stayed stuck, dreaming but never doing anything about it.

But after nine years of thinking, stewing, and staying stuck and miserable, life intervened. Doug got laid off. He walked into the house carrying a cardboard box. "How was work, honey?" his wife asked, cradling their youngest in her arms.

"I got laid off," he said. "And I'm not going back to work, Sal."

"Excuse me?"

Sally was pregnant with their third child. They had loans to repay. Sally was working part-time as an account manager, but they needed his salary to make ends meet.

He answered, "I hate what I do. I'm going to start my own business." Doug had admitted it. He had just laid it on the line.

Sally answered: "No, you are not going to start a business. You are going to get a job. You've been reading too many goddamn Robert Kiyosaki books. That crap about flipping real estate and pursuing your passion—that's for people whose kids are grown up. You need to get a freaking job."

Doug put his arms around Sally and said, "I know you are scared, so am I. But I am tired of being so unhappy. Will you help me? I need to do this, and I need you, Sal." That's the line that will melt anyone: *Will you help me? I need you.*

Doug told Sally he would run numbers in the morning to see how long they could last on unemployment and how they could cut expenses. He promised he would give her a drop-dead date to have a business producing money or else he'd get a job. She let out a muffled, and very unconvincing, "Okay." He squeezed her a little tighter and said, "Thank you, Sal." And then he kissed her on the forehead and walked into the den to start figuring out their monthly budget and making calls to meet with people and ask for advice.

Having that discussion with someone who really matters to you, especially if your decisions will also affect him or her, is extremely hard. As you think about it, a looming sense of danger arrives, a feeling that the consequences of telling the truth will be too high. But you're not looking at it the right way. The danger has already arrived. Your life is slowly driving you crazy anyway. Whatever security you think you're holding onto is totally outweighed by the slow, depressing misery that comes from feeling stuck. You need to recognize that the risk of moving toward your dreams is much lower than the slow, everyday punishment you inflict on yourself by suppressing your dreams. And if the person you're speaking to really cares about you, then she will do her best to help you if you ask her, even if she doesn't love the idea at first.

Once you start making real connections by saying what's really on your mind, and sharing with people what you really want, you'll start to feel different. You won't feel exposed—you'll feel expansive. You'll start to feel as if you're really in touch with the world in a different way. As if you belong there.

Discover a *More Powerful You*

AN emerging field of study called "network science" is now asserting that all kinds of behavior such as obesity, smoking, sleeplessness among teens, drug use, happiness, and divorce is passed through social networks. Behavior is contagious. Dr. Nicholas Christakis, a Harvard professor who studies health and social networks, caused a firestorm a couple of years ago by statistically proving that your friends and friends-of-friends are making you fat. In fact, your chance of becoming obese increases 57 percent if you have a friend who's obese. Your chance of getting divorced increases by 147 percent. This has been proven true for loneliness and all sorts of social and personal behaviors.

Look at your circle of friends—are they a good influence or a bad one? Given that behavior is contagious, if you keep relationships with people who match your goals in terms of lifestyle and health—in other words, people you truly connect with, for all the right reasons—you're much more likely to adopt their behaviors, too. That's one more reason to learn how to seek out, and hang out with, people who can help you move toward the things you want. Upgrade your friends, and you will upgrade your life.

Identify one person who has what you want or has done what you would like to try, and reach out and ask that person for help.

CHAPTER EIGHT

Step 4:
Zoom Out and Create a Map

Now that you've overcome your embarrassment and gone public with your desire, I've got some good news. You are very lucky. You live at a time unlike any other. Your grandparents and your parents did not have the tools that you have at your disposal. If they wanted to change their lives, it took a lot of money, a new degree, and very probably a move across the country. In practice, most of them didn't have a chance in hell of changing anything. They were stuck in the same job, the same circle of friends, and the same town for most of their adult lives. The only thing that changed was the seasons.

But the world has changed enormously since then. Unlike your parents, you have exactly what you need to get what you desire. Because of technology, the proliferation of information on the Web, hyperconnectivity, and oversharing through social media, you have access to everything you need. There's a way to get whatever you want without requiring money, a degree, or a move across the country. And no matter how crazy, far-fetched, or scary your desire feels, there is someone on the planet who has done it and has probably blogged about it, been featured in some magazine, or joined an online group to help himself get it done. There is a living, breathing example of the life you imagine out there right now, and you are going to use that person and all the tools at your disposal to help yourself get that life.

Discover a *More Powerful You*

A cyclist produces a wake of air behind himself. This wake has vortices and creates a little wind that actually moves along with the cyclist. If you get behind him and follow his lead, the wake pushes you forward. This is called drafting. Scientists have proven that when you draft, you exert 30 percent less effort than the person you are tailing. Same is true in life. If it has never been done before, you will bring a hell of a lot more angst and fear to your effort. If you know you are following behind someone else who's blazing the trail and creating a wake for you, it will be easier. Identify two people who are doing or have done what you would like to do. Then learn as much as you can about them and how they got where they are.

People have quit jobs, become single parents, found love late in life, started magazines, gone back to school, invented a product, lost 150 pounds, started a company, self-published a novel, built confidence, reinvented themselves, survived an affair, healed their family, and quit drug addiction. Whatever you desire exists. The hard work is already done. Someone else has blazed a trail and you can just follow his or her lead and draft behind. Your only real job is to focus on finding that trail and pushing through whatever self-defeating talk comes up in your head.

You Need a Map

Maybe until now you've been wandering through your life without any real direction. You're like a stubborn driver lost on back roads in a place you don't know. You have no idea where you are, so you obsessively focus on what is right in front of you. There are signs on all the roads, but you have no context to know which ones are right. So you take whichever turn "feels" right, hoping to somehow find your path on just luck and gut feeling alone. Of course, most of the time that just leaves you even more lost.

And just like any stuck driver, the only way you're ever going to get where you want to be is if you use a map and zoom out to get some perspective on where you stand in relation to the life you want. Think of a program like Google Maps. You input where you are, where you want to be, and suddenly you not only have a map but a much larger perspective on where your journey fits into the world. You can zoom in to examine important details, or zoom out for the big picture. Anytime you get lost on your trip, you can just glance down at the map and see how to keep moving in the right direction.

You might not know it, but you can do the same thing with your own life. Google won't do it for you, but that's okay because it isn't hard. The thing to remember is that somewhere out there, what you desire exists, so you need to figure out where you stand in relation to it. Seeing the gap will help you understand how to close it. Until now, you haven't been able to see a way to get what you desire. You need a map to help you break down the path between where you are right now and where you want to be. If you don't have a map, even if you're fully committed to change, chances are you'll get lost.

How to Make a Map

Your map will look like an aerial view of a river with a lot of rocks. You are on one side and what you want is on the other. Your job is to jump across all the rocks to get to the other side.

Every rock in the river represents an action: a person to reach out to, a meeting to attend, a business plan to write, a task you must complete, classes to take, research to do, a website to build, training to get, conversations you must have.

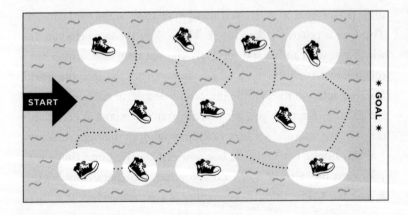

Discover a *More Powerful You*

ONLINE at www.melrobbins.com/map you can download free templates to help you create your own map. You can also find examples of maps that have been built for making a career change, getting into a committed relationship, losing weight, and getting out of debt. You can share ideas with other people, and get advice on what circles to add.

Before you start to fill in the circles on the map, which represent the rocks you'll be leaping onto in your journey, there are four guidelines you must follow:

►1. Do not fill this out in a logical order.

Your map is not a step-by-step set of directions. It is a tool for giving you the perspective you need to start getting creative about getting what you want. A map does not say, "Turn here, then after five miles, turn right on this specific road." Those are logical, linear directions.

The problem with directions like that is they are too rigid. What if you miss a turn? What if there's construction, and one of the roads you were told to take is blocked off? If all you have are a rigid set of step-by-step instructions, the moment you hit an unexpected snag or make a single mistake, you'll be lost.

Your map is much more useful than that. With a map, if you miss a turn or can't take a path you'd planned on, you can just glance down and figure out another way to go. A rigid set of directions gives you one way to get where you're going—but a map offers a huge array of options, and the perspective to help you choose which one is right for you in each moment. How many times have you printed out step-by-step directions online and they've been wrong? If you have a map you can pick your own route and navigate around detours!

Your dreams are like a massive, cross-country road trip. If you tried to plot out every single turn and road you'd take, inevitably you'd get lost. You'd hit some snag along the way—like an accident, or traffic, or some confusing signs, or a detour—and all of a sudden your carefully plotted directions would be useless. A good map allows you to adapt to whatever obstacles you hit and keep on moving. If you're getting bored of the interstate, change the route along the way. The options are endless when you have a map to guide you.

The same is true about the path of life. Things never happen in the order you plan on. Instead, when you start rolling and things are just "clicking," weird things happen, coincidences appear, serendipity occurs, and opportunities come out of nowhere. You want that to happen!

Use this explorer's philosophy to fill in your map in a random order as things pop into your head. Resist your urge to make it "right" or a straight line. Life is not linear and does not work in some perfect order. So stop trying to make your map some nice, neat step-by-step directions. A map just covers the entire landscape and in doing so allows you to lean in and explore.

► **2. This is a creative brainstorming exercise.**

You must expand your thinking here, not shrink it. To make your map, just list the things you need to do. When you find yourself knocking things off the list, you are shrinking your thinking. Stop it. *Everything* that comes to mind that you "should" do goes on the map. Anything that is remotely related to this thing you desire (or even that you just think might be), put it on the map.

A map doesn't come with a timeline or a clock, so don't worry about how long things might take or when you might find the time to do them. If it needs to happen at some point in the next five years, so be it—just write it down.

►3. Come at your desire from all different directions.

If you lost the keys to your house and had to get inside, how might you do it? The front door is not the only option. You'd check all the windows, you'd check the back door, the side door, and the bulkhead to the basement. You'd see if the garage door was open or if there was an open window on the second story. Same is true with what you want. There are lots of ways to get what you want. See if you can't think of as many ways as possible to "break in" to the thing you want. If you consider some of the top chefs in the world, they all come from very different backgrounds. Some went to culinary institutes, others grew up in restaurants, and some just started on the line and worked their way up. You can arrive at the same place, via very different routes. Have fun trying to plot as many as you can to what you desire. **Create at least four different routes.**

Your map has one purpose: to help guide you to what you want in life. It will show you all the landmarks, the milestones, and the possible paths that you can take and give you limitless options on how to keep moving forward. It is also completely expandable as you start off, learn new things, and want to change direction slightly. How you decide to navigate it is up to you. You are simply labeling the landscape around your dreams.

►4. No shortcuts.

Shortcuts in life never work, yet we all try to take them: "I've had it, I'm losing weight. From now on I'm only going to eat grapefruit

and cabbage!" "That's it. My boss is such an unbearable ass, I quit."
"I'm never dating another man as long as I live!" These drastic steps
are a way to avoid the real work of creating a lasting, sustainable
change in your life.

But they never work. The grapefruit-and-cabbage diet is going
to make you miserable. You'll last three days before you break down
and binge on Ben & Jerry's. When you quit your job, you'll feel like
a superstar for about ten minutes and then panic will set in when
you realize you don't have health insurance—which will mean that
instead of getting the job you really want, you'll be scrambling to
find anything you can just to keep food on the table. Doing something rash and drastic is not sustainable.

That's because change is not just a perfect sound bite with an
exit stage left, or a complete overhaul, or a 180-degree shift complete
with burning rubber. Change is the slow accumulation of details.
Change is checking off days on a calendar. Change is waking up
on a morning just like any other and finally feeling different, as if
you've got something to look forward to, because you've taken back
control of a small part of your life. Big leaps and drastic measures
rarely work in real life. Innovation occurs by making small movements that add up to huge change. You just need to remember that
you're in it for the long haul, and your success does not depend on
any one act. Your change will be the accumulation of a whole series
of decisions. If you find yourself spinning and it feels like a horrible
struggle to change a part of yourself, you might need to back off
and reassess.

Maybe you are trying to change too much at once. For example,
if you have always had the habit of sleeping in on weekends, rarely
exercising, and watching movies every night, a cold-turkey switch-
over to early morning runs and reading Russian novels every night

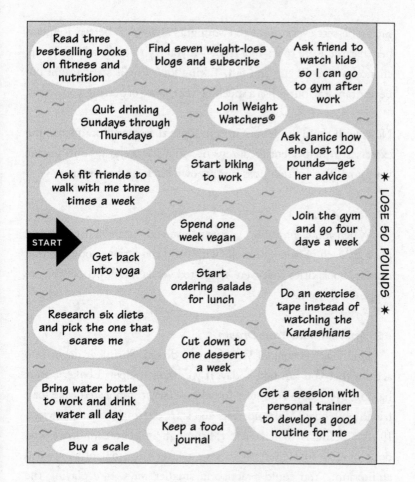

is going to be tough. You can't engineer a full brain transplant and simply become someone else and expect that to just stick. After a week or two, your old self is going to come back twice as hard.

As you fill out your map, remember that lots of little circles beats one giant circle. If you've got a major sweet tooth, writing "I'll never eat dessert again" is not a good circle. Writing "Go from eating dessert every night to two nights a week" is better. Remember that these are rocks in a river—if you try to make a huge jump, chances are you'll slip and fall. Taking lots of little steps might not be as dramatic, but it has a much better chance of getting you across.

Now, with these guidelines in mind, use these seven brainstorming exercises to help identify dozens of actions you can take to pursue your goal. Each action goes into its own circle on your map.

► 1. Take Advice

When you went public, you were given advice and a list of things to do by each person you spoke with. Add the actions you were told to take, book titles that were suggested, or names of people you are supposed to contact.

► 2. Approximate Your Dream

Find tiny versions of your faraway dream. Shrink it down into actions that you can take today. If you want to open a bakery, start baking, every day. Volunteer to bake a crazy, complicated cake for a friend's birthday. Make up fliers and start offering catering services. If your desire is to have a breakthrough in your confidence, you don't have to force yourself to give a speech in front of a crowded auditorium. You could practice in smaller ways, like playing the "eye-contact game" and looking four strangers in the eyes a day with a warm smile, signing up for Toastmasters, subscribing to iTunes university lectures on confidence, or just making a habit of asking the cashier at Dunkin' Donuts how his or her day is going.

There are small ways to do what you hope to on a large scale, right now. Today. With no money, no training, no long-term commitment, figure out how you can approximate your dream and add those actions to your map.

►3. Follow the Leader

Next, track down information about someone who has done what you desire. Who in the world has or does what you wrote down? It can be someone famous, someone you know, or someone you know of.

Businesses use this tool all the time. It's called "best practices." You look at successful companies and model what they are doing. Countless business school case studies have been written about Nike, Apple, Google, and GE. And every business plan that's written to raise money has a "competitive landscape" analysis that looks at every other business in a related category to the one being started. Smart businesspeople analyze what other companies are doing right and what they are doing wrong and use that information to help themselves map out a plan to be even more successful. You are going to use the same tool to analyze the best practices of human beings who have or do what you desire.

If there isn't someone who has the exact thing that you want, then pick a blend of people. Here's how to do it: Just learn as much about that person and from that person as you can to help get what you want. They hold invaluable clues. Follow her on Twitter. Friend her on Facebook. If you don't know her, send her a message about what you are up to and ask for her help. Google her and learn as much as you can about her. What are the things that she did to get what you want? Does she have a degree? What relationships does she have? What risks did she take? What hobbies does she pursue? Whatever she does, do the same thing. Everything that you learn as you do your research goes onto your map.

One of the most respected and cited social psychologists in the world, Timothy Wilson, says that the classic twelve-step tenet of "Fake it till you make it" may be one of the best pieces of advice you can follow. Think about it: One of the foremost experts on how people think says just act like the person you want to become. When you act the part and *pretend* to be a better person, your mind actually begins to operate differently. You start to activate new behaviors in your unconscious. Keep it up over time, and you slowly end up becoming the person you're imitating. With a map to constantly remind you of what actions to take—you'll surely succeed.

► 4. Get a Ph.D.

Adopt the attitude that you are going to give yourself your own Ph.D. in the subject by learning as much as you can. Spend several weeks becoming an expert on what you desire. Add each of these actions to your map:

1. Perform research about the thing that you want. For example, if you want to stop feeling like roommates in your marriage and reconnect again, Google the topic. If you want to stop smoking, same thing.
2. Sign up for a class, a webinar, or a podcast series on the topic.
3. Find at least four books and seven blogs to read.
4. Whatever you learn in your research that sounds like interesting or scary actions to take, add to the map.
5. Whatever advice or assignments you stumble upon as you read up on the topic, add them to your map.

► 5. Join a Group

What groups, trade shows, conferences, associations, online courses, lectures, or events exist that relate to what you want? Find them and make joining them and attending a meeting or event an action item on your map. There's no faster way to accelerate this process of changing your life than to surround yourself with people who do the same thing that you are interested in. You cannot underestimate the power of proximity when it comes to forming connections. In 1974, researchers conducted a study of a Maryland state police training academy. At the academy, both dorm rooms and classrooms were assigned in alphabetical order. Six months after their arrival, cadets were asked to name their three closest friends. Ninety percent of the cadets named the person whose last name was next to theirs. Why? Proximity. If you sit next to someone every day, you tend to form a bond. A similar study held true for bench scientists; they named the person sitting next to them. In dormitories, another study detailed that you were exponentially more likely to be friends with the person living across the hall than with someone at the end of the hall.

When it comes to connecting with someone, a few feet can matter a lot. That's the power of proximity. When you are near someone all the time, you find yourself connecting with him or her more easily. You form closer bonds because of the proximity of being near each other.

Discover a *More Powerful You*

I'VE noticed that my social life has changed dramatically based on where my kids are located any given year. When my daughters were attending a local preschool, we would socialize with the other families who had kids there. It wasn't because they were our favorite people or even who we wanted to hang out with—it was because of proximity. You'd be picking up your daughter and pass someone in the parking lot. "Hey, what are you doing this weekend? Want to come over for a barbecue?" Now that the kids are older, we find ourselves making plans on the sidelines of soccer fields and karate lessons. The reason—proximity. You tend to gel with people who are standing right next to you. Use that to your advantage. Join groups and stand next to people who are doing what you desire. The proximity alone will exponentially increase your chance of clicking with them. Make an effort to expand your social circle beyond the people that you are proximate to. There are lots of cool people you know that you don't see nearly enough. They just aren't standing next to you right now.

If you surround yourself with like-minded people, your efforts to reach your goal will be rewarded. Joining those groups that relate to what you desire, attending their functions, and standing next to those folks you want to meet must go on the map as well. And while you are at it, add joining a committee of the group to the map. That will guarantee you proximity with the people you need to know because you'll be working shoulder to shoulder with them on the committee.

► 6. Innovate

Take a step back and check out each one of the circles on your map. Can you innovate any of them? If so, add the action you would take to your map. Innovation is about taking a step to the right or left; it's about experimenting.

Chris and his business partner, Jonathan, did this with their business, StoneHearth Pizza. Their core business was thin-crust pizza using ingredients from local farms around New England. Their goal was to sell as many pizzas as possible. They had three restaurants in the Boston metropolitan area, but they were always innovating the method they used to get pizzas to the public. They started with dine-in only. Once they nailed that, they made a small innovation—offering delivery.

Then they printed a catering menu. Next they were volunteering to do events. That innovation required them to figure out how to cook their pizzas outside, so they experimented. After weeks of work, they determined that a massive grill was the best bet. Their pizzas sold like hotcakes at a music festival. Grilled pizzas made them see the next obvious innovation: they should sell them wholesale to grocery stores. A couple of hundred networking meetings later, small innovations have led them to contracts with Whole Foods and other nationwide supermarket chains, where you can now find their refrigerated pizzas advertised as "great on the grill." Their wholesale business was born—all through one small innovation at a time.

For every circle on your map, can you think of one small innovation that you could make to push it forward in a new direction? Put that action on the map.

► 7. Blow Up Obstacles

List all the obstacles between you and the thing that you want. Add all of the obstacles that you see to your map. However, you will write them down as follows: "Get advice on how to work around the fact that . . ." Then list the obstacle. By writing it down as a task, you force yourself to figure out how to push through the obstacle and tap the power of the people you meet to help you figure out a solution.

How a Good Map Works

If you design them properly, maps work because they help you break down the gap between you and what you desire into step-by-step actions. By breaking things down into smaller chunks, it will be much easier for you to actually take action in the first place. You can find this advice everywhere from business school case studies to kitchen table discussions—we all know that the only way to eat an elephant is one bite at a time. If your goals remain too huge you'll get overwhelmed by the perceived distance between where you are and where you want to be. So you give up. By getting all the small step-by-step actions down on paper, in *one* place, you'll be able to push yourself to pick away at it.

Discover a *More Powerful You*

YOU can find endless examples of this "continuous-improvement" of process theory in the business world. Both the *kaizen* (Japanese word for "improvement") and GE's version, Six-Sigma, consulting methods focus on making tiny incremental changes to improve the efficiency of any business process. They focus on the process, knowing that if you make changes there you will realize tremendous results. Whether it is how employees log time or cap bottles on a production line, if you break down the process, you can find ways to improve it. UPS is serious about this stuff. Recently it told its drivers to avoid left turns because they take longer than right turns and to "carry the ignition key on the pinkie finger of their nondominant hand so they don't lose time rummaging through their pockets." Breaking down your goals into small chunks is what experts at taking action do in the business world. For writers, that's the tried-and-true advice: Forget about the great American novel, just sit down and write one page, every single day. Or for you dieters out there, don't eat a whole chocolate-chip cookie, eat a single chocolate chip. What could you break down in your life?

Psychologists and business consultants who specialize in "goal-theory" unilaterally recommend that you start off with goals that are attainable—breaking your goals down makes them much more so. Those early wins build confidence and stamina. That's why you give a kid a bike with training wheels. Let him at least learn to pedal and brake before we make him wrestle the force of gravity. There's no debate that breaking things into tiny little actions and improvements allows you to move forward.

The moment I realized how powerful this concept was was when I started breaking down my exercise routine. For years I was a runner. I had completed several marathons with other moms in my town. I also went to yoga classes frequently with this same group of friends. I got used to having to carve out two hours to exercise. Whether I was going to a yoga class, the gym, or taking a long run, when I added in the time to dress, the drive, the exercise routine, and shower postworkout, it was at least two hours. As my career got busier and my kids got older (and more demanding) I ran out of time. I began to feel like exercising was impossible with my responsibilities as a mom and businesswoman.

And then it struck me that I was making a classic mistake. I was telling myself, "I have to either find two hours or not exercise at all." But what if I stopped thinking in terms of one massive commitment and broke down my exercise routine into smaller, more attainable chunks? What if I just ran two miles and did twenty crunches a day? That would only take thirty minutes. I could get in the exercise and get my work done in time to hang with my kids. The process of breaking things into smaller pieces turned a seemingly unattainable goal into something I could at least make some progress on.

If you've always wanted to be a musician, don't think of it in terms of "I must practice five hours a day and take a million classes." Because chances are, you're not going to have five free hours a day, and you're not going to have the money for all those classes. So break it down into smaller chunks. Maybe you take one class, and maybe you practice one hour a day. Whatever you can do. Remember that it is always better to take lots of small actions than to get intimidated by one massive action and end up not doing anything at all.

By now your map should be overcrowded with things to do. Good. As you move from circle to circle, you will learn things and have more actions to include on your map. That is to be expected. Your map will get more and more detailed as you take action. As new ideas strike—just add them to the map. The more you have to do, the less likely you will stop to analyze everything to death and paralyze yourself.

Pull back and check out the big picture right now. That thing that you want—it is possible. If you were to do everything that is now on your map, you would get what you want. There is a way to have what you want. It is staring you in the face. There is just one thing between you and having it—you. People who have what they want push through and start taking action. They turn off the TV and start following their map. People who are stuck stare at their map and stand still. It doesn't matter whether you feel like it or not—just do it. Begin. Make your move.

CHAPTER NINE

Step 5:

Lean In to Change

So now you have your map to help guide you and keep you moving in the right direction. You know exactly what you have to do. But chances are when you sit down to do it, your resistance will rear its ugly head again and your brain will start doing everything it can to sabotage you. You will soon feel paralysis kicking in. Your mind will start to trick you. With your path all laid out in front of you, you will go into uncertainty hyperdrive and you will convince yourself that you don't have a clue what to do first.

Your brain is sensing a change in routine brewing so it starts what it does best—analyzing, thinking, considering the situation. If you aren't immediately empowered and taking action you'll start feeling a little chicken about the whole thing or a bit annoyed that it is going to be so much work. If you don't push through, you will soon be trapped inside your head: *Why am I doing this? Am I good enough to be doing this? Shouldn't I be doing something else? Isn't someone going to get mad about me doing this? I don't have the time to do this. I need to raise money. Who am I kidding? I can't do all this. If Jack had simply proposed, I wouldn't have to be signing up for this dumb speed-dating thing. If my stupid company hadn't laid me off, I wouldn't have to do this.*

Your thoughts will spin off into endless circles, and meanwhile your life will go nowhere. But this is all just noise. **Whenever your brain starts jabbering away like this, it is a sign to just keep going.**

This is the moment. You will either stay stuck or you will push through. You must remember there is no "right" move to make. You can pick anything on your map to do right now, and it will be a step forward. There is no risk. So when your brain tries to look for a rigid step-by-step set of instructions, just remember that every single circle on your map takes you one step closer to what you desire. Every time you find yourself overanalyzing your choices, stop yourself, pick anything on your map, and push through.

Activation Energy Required

To get what you want you need to form an instant connection between what you want to do and actually doing it. The speed of that connection is critical to your success. Remember the term "activation energy"—it's the amount of force required to take that first step. To create a new habit of action, the amount of force required in you is enormous. The longer you wait, the more you think and the faster you lessen the impulse to take action. It loses its energy very quickly. Think about the force it takes to get up instead of hitting the snooze, or the force it takes to get you to walk out the door and exercise. When you hit snooze or blow off a jog for surfing the Web it's because it took too much activation energy to force yourself out the door.

So here's a rule to help get you moving: Pick any circle on your map and begin in five seconds or less. Wait any longer, and your habitual thinking will kick in and you'll do nothing. The longer you delay, the more likely you will do nothing. The faster you act, the faster you start killing your habit of doing nothing. It takes practice, but this is the golden rule. Think of all action like launching a rocket. The five seconds is your countdown to launch. If that rocket doesn't leave the pad within five seconds, it's not going anywhere.

Taking action that fast will feel like the wrong thing to do. But that's just your resistance talking, begging you to hit snooze again. Remember, we are talking about decisions that are on your map, which means that by definition, any of them is going to help you move toward your desire. Overanalyzing them isn't going to do anything for you. Not one of them is a bad idea or the "wrong" choice. The only wrong choice is to do nothing.

So stop thinking. Just look at your map, pick something, and do it. If you still can't choose, just close your eyes and pick at random. Whatever you pick, that's the next thing you should be doing. And notice that nowhere on your map is a circle that says "Waste time analyzing this to death." There's a good reason for this—overthinking it is not going to get you any closer to what you want.

Tom's drinking started when he got injured at work and started self-medicating with a Jack Daniel's and Coke, which led to Jack on the rocks, which led to Jack drinking through the day to keep from feeling the pain. He was what some would call a "functioning alcoholic." He could keep a job, drive a car, hold a conversation, but was never without alcohol. Tom bumped into Anna, an old classmate from high school, at a local bar one night, and soon they were seeing each other. Anna thought Tom was just a "partier" and had no clue about the true extent of his problem until they started living together.

He'll never forget the day he learned that Anna was pregnant.

He tried to get sober then, but didn't. When the baby was born, a little girl named Emma, he quit booze for a week and then went right back to it. Anna tried to get a handle on his drinking. She planned an intervention with his family and told him to go to detox or never see their daughter again. He went to detox, but was back drinking within months of his release. They fought all the time, and that just made him drink to tune her out. Eventually, he told himself it would be easier if he just disappeared. So he did. Tom's mother stayed in contact with Anna, so he got spotty reports and occasionally a school photo.

Four years later, Tom got sober. Every day, he tortured himself with the thought of seeing his daughter again. He remarried a woman named Joan, and they had a two-year-old daughter, Charlotte, together. But having a new daughter just filled Tom with more and more regret about Emma. The gravity of his decision to walk out weighed on him more heavily each day. Not a day went by that Tom didn't think about Anna and his daughter Emma. But despite his regret, Tom did nothing. He thought constantly about calling Anna but had no idea what he would say. He thought about what Anna must have told Emma about him—or worse, that maybe she hadn't said anything.

Tom's situation sounds a lot more serious than, for example, Lisa, who is merely trying to push herself to start a granola business. But it is not. Both Tom and Lisa feel stuck for the same reason. They want something and they are doing nothing to pursue it. Doing nothing is making them feel bad about themselves, feel stuck in their lives, and with each day that passes what they want feels further away. They both need to do the same thing. They need to push through the mental bullshit and take action.

You are the same. You know what you want and all that's keeping you from having it is your fear. **Everything you desire is on** the other side of your fear. If you push through, you will get it. If you do nothing, you'll get nothing. Because the activation energy is so great, you think the action itself has serious ramifications. But it doesn't. Everything on your map is a tiny, tiny little step toward your dream. You don't need to quit your job. You won't lose everything you have. Anna may not want Tom to meet Emma, but she isn't going to pull a rifle on him. The stakes are simply not as high as you have inflated them to be.

Every day Tom thinks about how he can be a part of Emma's life. He thinks about introducing Emma to her half sister. Wherever he goes—the grocery store, the mall, the pharmacy—he imagines bumping into Anna and Emma. What would he do or say? He longs to be free from this tremendous burden of regret. But the activation energy required to take that first step is too much for him. He's delayed it for so long—it feels impossible to take action. The steps are obvious, and by now you should know them.

1. **Face the truth.** Tom is not fine with this situation. He needs to make amends.
2. **Admit what you want.** Tom wants a relationship with Emma.
3. **Go public.** Tom needs to tell his sponsor, his wife, Joan, his mother, and his close friends and ask for guidance and advice.
4. **Make a map.** There are hundreds of actions that Tom could take to bring him one step closer to his daughter and to peace. Tom could write a letter, make a phone call, ask his mother to help broker a meeting, send monthly support checks, see a therapist.

There's only one way for Tom to solve this. The moment he thinks (as he does every day) of writing a letter, he must act within five seconds. He worries about what to say, but we all know actions speak louder than words. And there are only a few words that he needs to say: *I am sorry. I love you. I made mistakes. I am sober. Meet your sister. Please forgive me. I'll support you. I'm your dad.* As he sits down to write, he needs to put pen to paper within five seconds. As soon as he finishes, he needs to seal and address the envelope within five seconds. And then he needs to drive to a public mailbox and drop it in, immediately.

Lean In

Any move you pick will push you toward what you want, but finding the activation energy to make that move can feel enormously difficult. So how, in that moment of fear, regret, panic, and longing do you force yourself to make a move? You lean in.

Leaning in is a philosophy about change that will change your life. To get an object that is standing still to move in a new direction and start rolling—that first bit of motion is just the most subtle shift in weight. It's not a jump. It's not a leap. It's simply a small motion. When you lean toward the thing you want, gravity takes over, momentum builds, and you begin to become a more powerful you.

Seth's life was a mess. He'd gotten married too young to a woman he didn't love, which lead to an affair, which lead to divorce before he was thirty. He felt as if his whole life up to then had been erased. He'd lost half his friends and half his money, and just about every idea that he had about what his life was going to be like was wrong. He had no idea what to do next. He was back at the beginning, only this time he had lost ten years and was alone. He used to be the only married guy people knew and now he was the only divorced one. He felt like he was going nowhere, and he hated the guy he'd become.

Seth was sick of himself and he had no real clue how to tackle the huge problems in his life. So he focused on making one small change to his screwed-up life, taking a single step to cope with a single problem. He'd always been afraid of heights. Sitting on a bar stool practically gave him vertigo. So he resolved to break out of that fear, change his routine, and do something he never thought he could. He decided to go skydiving.

Which was how, a few days later, he found himself wearing a blue jumpsuit, sitting on the floor of a little plane that sounded like it was powered by a rubber band, heading for eleven thousand feet. He started to think, *This is the stupidest idea I've ever had. I can't do this. I should just go home.* Truthfully, if he wasn't already strapped to the instructor, he would have bailed.

The doors slid open, the cables were attached, and it was time to act. Seth froze. The instructor said, "The $275 is for the ride up, the ride down is free. If you are going to do this, now is the time." But Seth didn't feel like jumping. He was scared to death. But with the wind whipping all around him he wondered, what would he be going home to? And in that instant the roar of the wind coming from the open plane fell silent in his mind. He quietly remembered that it was a Sunday afternoon and the only thing waiting for him at home was Chinese takeout and a knot in his stomach thinking about another Monday at a job he hated. Did he really want to be that guy anymore? The guy who let fear and regret rule his life? The guy who let divorce turn him into a worthless sad sack?

So he closed his eyes, adjusted his goggles, eased to the edge of the open plane door, and simply shifted his weight. He didn't leap from the plane like an action hero. He didn't do anything drastic. He just leaned in to the open sky and the chance that something might shift in his life and let gravity do the rest. And with that tiny action, everything changed. In that moment he stopped being the guy who was too scared to handle a risk, who never did anything interesting, who let his failures define him. He became someone else. Someone whose life wasn't over, but was just beginning.

You don't need to take a massive leap. All you need to do is lean in and see what happens next. Leaning into that open sky gave Seth a wild ride and one hell of a stomachache, but that choice to lean in, that small shift in weight and change in direction, changed his life forever because it put him in motion.

That is what leaning in is all about: taking the small action that will let your momentum take over and carry you forward. If your marriage has gone stale and you barely communicate with your spouse, the answer isn't to spend forever overthinking the "right" thing to do, nor is it to take some massive leap like moving to another state or demanding a divorce out of the blue. The answer is to pick some small action that will get the ball rolling, and just do it. Pick up the phone, call your spouse, and say, "I think we need to have a talk tonight." That's it. Or send a text that says "I miss how we used to be." It seems small, but that phone call or text means that when you see your spouse, you'll have a real conversation. And that conversation will open the door to new paths of action and ways to fix your marriage. And then don't stop there, do it again and again. It's about making that tiny push, and then letting gravity pull you through.

You've spent most of your adult years unlearning all the good stuff that you knew as a kid. When you were young, you lived to "lean in." The second you had an impulse to do something, you'd go do it, and then you'd let that carry you forward. You didn't spend hours agonizing over whether to ride your bike, and if so, where and for how long. You just hopped on the seat and started pedaling. Next thing you knew you'd be racing up and down the street, or exploring a new neighborhood, or riding to meet up with friends.

Which would inevitably lead to more fun activities. You didn't need a step-by-step plan. You just took action and let your momentum fill your day with fun things to do. Kids have unlimited momentum, but it often goes dormant as you get older. As an adult, you think you have to figure it all out before you even take one step.

Tom doesn't need to waste another second trying to figure out how Anna will react, because the truth is there's no way to know what she'll do. Tom just needs to do something to move forward and then figure it out. He is slowly rotting from the inside out worrying about the right way to do this. But in leaning in, there is no "right" way, there is only moving forward.

So look at your map. Pick anything to move to. Whatever you just picked on your map, do it now. You must lean in the direction of what you desire, and you have to do it right now. You cannot wait or your impulse will dry up. Tom cannot afford to wait one millisecond before he puts pen to paper and starts writing. If he waits, he'll talk himself out of it. But if he just writes it, he'll put himself in motion. Then the next step, addressing and sending it, will seem just a bit easier. And that will open up a path to other actions, from sending more letters to calling. It will all happen once he forces himself to take that first, seemingly tiny step of writing "Dear Anna . . ."

So send that e-mail. Pick up the phone. Sign up for that class. Commit and do it. What matters right now in this moment is that you push through your feelings and start moving. Take action and lean toward what you want without regard for how it will look or turn out. It is the smallest of actions, but internally it is going to feel wrong. Pushing through your paralysis and your excuses is very hard. And the more you fear the decision, the harder it will be to push through your fears and just lean in. Why do you think Tom has put off contacting Anna for three years? Because he is scared. It's the same reason you put off working on your résumé—you are scared. It's the same reason you won't put up a profile online—you are scared. The reason you don't take action is the same every time—you are scared.

All you have to do is pick something on the map and do it. It doesn't matter what you pick. This is the first time in your life when the order of things is irrelevant. Everything on your map will lead you toward the beacon. So there is no risk. You path is going to wind, and twist, so it doesn't matter whether you decide to call someone first, do research, find someone to learn about, or sign up to attend a meeting. Whatever you choose to do, you will instantly accomplish three things:

1. You will push through your resistance, your uncertainty, and your paralysis, which will loosen their hold on you going forward.
2. You will bring yourself one step closer to what you want.
3. You will move out of the "preparation" stage (which, if your brain had its way, would go on forever) and begin your journey. You will go from *thinking about* starting to lose weight, to starting to lose weight. You will go from *thinking about* starting to fix your marriage, to starting to fix your marriage. This shift is crucial.

When Tom sent the letter, he immediately wanted to take it back. He was overcome with fear of Anna's reaction. And Anna did respond, with a postcard saying "Go to hell." But, Tom realized, that wasn't such a big deal. So Anna was angry at him. He knew that already. He was no worse off for having sent his letter. And, he slowly realized, what Anna did didn't really matter. He had his map, and he knew what he wanted—to be a part of his daughter's life. So he took a step back and reminded himself that there were many paths on the map. So he added "Get advice on dealing with Anna" to his map, picked another circle, and decided to sit down and start writing in five seconds before his impulse to act dries up.

This time he wrote another note, but included a check for child support. Anna returned the check and wrote, "We don't need your money. Please don't contact me again." Tom felt defeated, but picked another circle and within five seconds called the house and left a message: "I know you hate me and I don't blame you. I am calling to make amends. The FedEx package that is arriving today has something very important inside. Please open it."

Inside he'd put a long letter about his experience getting sober, his regrets, and how much he has learned about fatherhood. He wrote to Anna about how his marriage and sobriety had changed him and that Emma had a half sister—Charlotte—who wanted to meet her. He suggested they go see a therapist to figure out how to orchestrate a meeting and included a photo of himself with Joan and their two-year-old daughter. Tom just leaned in again. And with each successive action, he found that reaching out seemed less and less radical, that once he'd gotten the ball rolling on getting in touch it was becoming easier to keep moving toward what he wanted.

Eventually Tom stopped fearing Anna's reaction and came to expect it. As long as he kept his ultimate goal in sight, he could keep pushing through and moving closer toward what he desired, a meeting with his daughter. It took seven letters, three phone calls, one tense meeting moderated by a social worker, and five months later, Tom got what he desired: he met his daughter Emma.

What you want may not seem as "high stakes" as what Tom wanted, but it is, because no matter what you really desire, if you don't take action to get it you are always going to feel unsatisfied. Whatever the specifics are of what you want, what is fundamentally at stake is your happiness.

This is how you become an expert at taking action. You ignore how you feel, you stop thinking, and you just *act*. It doesn't have to be a huge action. You just need to do something and start moving. And then you do it again and again and again, letting the momentum from each action carry you through to the next one. The faster you take action, the more likely you will follow through. This requires practice. You are going to build your stamina and eventually will go from being an expert at doing nothing, to becoming an expert at taking action.

Now that you've learned how to start getting what you want, I'm going to teach you to build the stamina you need to *keep* getting what you want.

Part III: *Finding the Stamina to Keep Getting What You Want*

If you take care of the small things, the big things take care of themselves. You can gain more control over your life by paying closer attention to the little things.

—EMILY DICKINSON

CHAPTER TEN

Push Through the Mental Walls
That Block Your Path

The work required to get what you want never ends. You might as well add it to your long list of things that will always need your attention: groceries, laundry, trimming various errant hairs, bathing, making your bed, dishes, toenails. Everything needs to be kept up—and so does your life. Soon this step-by-step method will become just as second nature as the way you fold your shirts. There's nothing quite so satisfying as folding that last piece of laundry, placing it on top of the basket of clean clothes, turning off the light, and knowing you are done folding laundry for the night. But even once that shirt is folded, are you done with laundry forever? Of course not. When will you ever get to stop doing laundry? Never. The dishes? Never. Getting out of bed in the morning? Never. Fixing dinner, brushing your teeth, shaving? Never. Your life is filled with things that you need to do every single day, just because you have to do them. The same is true with pushing yourself forward. The method you just learned to get yourself moving forward again is something you will do over and over and over again.

If you ever feel stuck, bored, or broken it is a sign that you need to broaden and build some new experiences into your life. You're just doing more of the same old stuff. When you get this signal, you take the same five steps I outlined in part 2:

- Face the truth that something is missing from your life and you've been avoiding dealing because it is easier to do nothing.
- Admit what you really want.
- Go public, tell three people, and ask for advice.
- Create a map.
- Lean toward what you want. Then lean in again.

That is the basic anatomy of going from feeling stuck to taking action. And you will repeat this process over and over again throughout your life. Remember the activation energy it takes to push a car from a stop to a roll? That's the level of resistance you are dealing with when you get started. It's a huge load, which is why we've spent the entire book thus far teaching you how to muster up the force to get your life moving with that initial push through your fears and resistance to change. Once that car starts to roll, you still need to push. It will just be easier. After you have followed the method in part 2, your life should be moving forward in a new and exciting direction. You won't feel blah, bored, or broken down—you will feel in control and proud of yourself for pushing through.

Now let's walk you down what will soon be a familiar path. Now that you are awaking to all kinds of cool stuff you could be doing, new ideas, new people, and new experiences will flood into your life. You'll be walking down the street, noticing details you'd always ignored before, giving yourself a boost by making eye contact with strangers, on your way to talk to someone your friend said you should meet to help you reach your goal, and suddenly you'll have an epiphany. You want to become a chef, or a writer, or an entrepreneur, or a designer, or a forest ranger, or an actress, or start a nonprofit. This realization awakens all your past interests and dreams. Everything lines up in one shining sense of purpose. Of course, then you start to think that your idea is never going to work. It seems too crazy. It's going to require major changes in your life.

But since you've read this book you know that all these thoughts are just brain propaganda. You recognize these thoughts and feelings as lame tricks your brain is trying to use to keep you superglued to the rails of life. You smile confidently. *Nice try, but I'm not falling for it.* And you push through. You make a map. You approximate ways to take action on this great idea to change your life. You fill up the circles and have a ball challenging your mind to come up with various ways to innovate, attack from different angles to get what you want. You lean in and start to chip away at this dream. This is the golden rule for any kind of effort: to keep from getting discouraged, take on practical, immediate tasks that will slowly add up to some kind of meaningful change. Right?

Well . . . sorta. It's certainly how you break down those huge dreams of yours and coax yourself to push through fear and get started. You can logically convince yourself that if the steps are really tiny you can do it. But the truth is, if you just keep your head down and try to chip away at it, you will start doubting your dream and eventually you will talk yourself out of pushing forward. Your mind will start to convince you that these actions are pointless and the effort isn't getting you anywhere meaningful. Or you'll hear the word *no* too many times or fail to see the results stack up fast enough. Eventually, you'll abandon your map and your small steps and you'll be right back where you started: feeling stuck. You want to head this off before it happens.

What you're missing at this point is stamina. Tapping into the powerful you is what is required to stop feeling stuck. But eventually small progress isn't going to feel satisfying. You'll get bored and discouraged. Without accelerating your pace, you will start slacking off and only doing the actions that "feel" the easiest. That won't change your life. You'll choose the actions that take the least time and can be done in secret. You'll send an e-mail instead of picking up the phone. Tom will ask his mother to pick up Emma on the nights he has her for visitation, so he doesn't have to deal with Anna. Harold will bum a cigarette from someone—and tell himself that since he didn't buy the pack himself, it's not *really* smoking. Stephanie will see the toilet seat up in the bathroom, and after three months of marriage counseling and working at it, lose her mind and send Aaron a nasty text. Alison will sign up for Toastmasters but chicken out on going.

Making some quiet, secret commitment to take an online course helped you get rolling in the beginning, but eventually it becomes *too* easy. Googling the thought to death no longer leads to action. You read blogs from people who are doing the same thing and feel discouraged instead of e-mailing for advice like you used to. You read Wikipedia articles and find online courses about your dream. Inevitably you will get discouraged as you realize how far away the goal really is.

You need to train yourself to develop stamina and you need some easy, foolproof metacognition tricks, like those kids used in the marshmallow test to push through any setbacks or mind tricks that you encounter. Mental walls are just as dangerous as dead-ends in the real world, because they make you want to chuck it all. The worst thing you could do now that you've started rolling forward is give up. That sets into motion a whole series of additional mental hurdles that you create and need to overcome: embarrassment, failure, and resignation. You want to avoid those. There are five mental walls that you will hit as you try to get what you want. They are:

1. Feeling rejected
2. Feeling overwhelmed
3. Feeling unmotivated
4. Feeling like a fraud
5. Feeling discouraged

Dealing with Rejection and Setbacks

With your first burst of momentum, you will rack up a couple of fast wins and then you may hit a couple of walls and feel like everything crashes and burns. You know the feeling all too well.

It's your first few weeks on the *drink-bitter-cranberry-juice-and-only-eat-raw starvation diet* that has made you lose eight pounds a week for the first two weeks. But by the third week of trying to sustain yourself on a natural diuretic you are now dehydrated and starving and the weight is not coming off as fast. Even though you are down sixteen pounds you feel like a failure and think about throwing in the towel on the whole diet thing.

Or maybe you think it's shaping up to be a perfect day. You landed a client, or nailed a job interview, organized your first support group for moms with autistic kids, or got a green light on a project that you've been waiting for. It's time to celebrate. No sooner have you laid down your credit card on an expensive dinner for you and your spouse then you get an e-mail the next day. "We're starting to rethink our options, and it's probably not going to work." In a few days, you have gone from feeling flush to concluding that the world has just ended.

Whether you're trying to lose weight or get into the school of your dreams, become an entrepreneur or work for a company, find love or end a relationship, land a dream job or save the money to go on a dream vacation—life has its ups and downs. When you go for what you want in life, ups and downs are exactly what you signed up for, and if you don't learn to ride the wave, the wave will crush you. The truth is that effort is always rewarded in some way. From my own experience, and what I've seen from others, I know this is true.

There will always be setbacks, so you must learn how to deal with them. When you hit an obstacle, you shouldn't be questioning yourself, you should just be figuring out the alternatives. You should be like water. Water doesn't reconsider its flow. If something gets in its way, it just moves around the obstacle. You need to adopt the same mentality. Now that you are rolling forward, I do not want you to come to a screeching halt. I follow a four-step program:

1. I allow myself twenty-four hours to be a complete mess. I gripe. I cry. I feel insecure. I make the people who rejected me entirely in the wrong (losers!) or I complain incessantly about the diet not working. I punch the wall. I exercise. Then it's out of my system and it's over.

2. The next morning it's time to move on. I remind myself of all the amazing things that I have accomplished and of the setbacks I have already found a way to overcome. Like the sixteen pounds I've lost already or the fact that I have two other clients who are onboard.

3. Then I create a reason in my mind for why this rejection is the best thing that could happen to me. How did it actually strengthen me? And if I can't think of a reason, I call my most over-the-top Pollyanna friend and get her to convince me of one. Don't discount this tactic. Science has proven that when a person

walks into a room with a high level of positive energy and an optimistic outlook, strangers in the same room get infected with the positivity.

4. Then I pull out my trusty map, I put where I am and what I want in the center, and I build out options from there—to go from this new spot, to the next one. I realize that I need to up the ante on exercise if I expect to see the results I want. The map reminds me of what I want and shows me that I'm still within the vicinity. As soon as I see options, I can take a deep sigh of relief and know that all that's between me and what I want is, well, me.

Jennifer graduated from college with a degree in English. She went straight to a master's program and was lucky enough to get a job teaching English at a local community college. For five years, she kept a full-time course load teaching writing fundamentals and American literature.

This would have been a dream come true for most English majors. The only problem for Jennifer was discovering that she hated to teach. Every new semester, she hoped that this time it would click. It never did. Her husband, also a professor, was extremely supportive and encouraged her to read books about finding her purpose and attend women's weekends designed to help her find her path.

After much soul searching and with the support of her husband, Jennifer decided that she would go back to school and become a doctor. She had always been interested in medicine, the sciences, and loved the idea of helping people. She spent three years, raking up debt and going to school full time. She hadn't taken her premed requirements during college, so here she was at the age of thirty-one doing it at an extension school of a local university. She took her MCATS and applied to eight medical schools.

One by one, the responses came in. Every last one of them was a rejection. After three and half years of weekends and evenings spent studying, not to mention the forty grand in tuition, she did not even get into one school. Now what? When you hit a brick wall, what do you do?

In Jennifer's case, she crumbled. She felt absolutely crushed. She couldn't even bring herself to call the schools to find out why she was rejected, because it was just too painful. And worse, she felt trapped. After all that money and effort spent pursuing a dream that hadn't materialized, plus her first experience teaching, which also hadn't ended well, she felt as if her options for moving forward had dried up. She gave up on the idea of becoming a doctor. With no clue what to do, she thought about becoming a writer. It wasn't exactly in line with her original dream, but at least it wouldn't mean tens of thousands of dollars in schooling.

Jennifer's reaction is pretty common. When you put a lot of time and energy into something and it doesn't work out, the temptation is to just blow everything up again and move in an entirely new direction. But don't move too fast. At least not before you go back to the method for getting unstuck and make a map. First of all, the next decision that you make has so much pressure attached to it that you will feel jinxed, and likely fail under the strain. When you fail, it's important not to carry that failure forward with you.

To move forward in the face of rejection, you need to take a small step from where you are right now. Remember your map with the stones in the river. Make a new one. Draw eighteen circles on a piece of paper. Put your original goal in the middle circle. Then write three reasons why you desired that goal in the first place.

In Jennifer's case, she put "be a medical doctor" in the center circle. Then under it she wrote three reasons for that desire—"I love the sciences," "I like helping people," and "I'm interested in wellness."

Now, in the remaining seventeen circles you are going to write down ways in which you could accomplish those three things without being a medical doctor.

As soon as Jennifer started thinking in this way, her mind-set changed. Rather than feeling completely lost, she started rattling off ideas: I could become a naturopathic physician, a nurse, a dialysis researcher, a nutritionist; work for a vitamin manufacturer; become a physician's assistant, a chemist specializing in diet, an RN for a relief mission; and so on. Where she had seen only a dead end, she now saw options.

Life will back you into a corner. The only way out is through. As soon as you see multiple ways to have what you want, you will push through. Remember to be like water. If something gets in your way, flow around it.

Dealing with a Sense of Being Overwhelmed

Having a ton of things to do can be both a good thing and a bad thing when you are making changes in your life. The days where everything just clicks tend to be the ones where you have a lot going on and a full plate of things to accomplish. Those are my favorite kind of days because they have a momentum and satisfaction all their own. As you are crossing things off the list, and shucking and jiving through your day, you feel the confidence boost because you're *a player* in life with a lot going on. Even if you can't do everything, the choice of what to do is entirely up to you, and you have lots of options.

But there's a flip side. Having so much to do can very easily turn from being empowering and exciting into being overwhelming.

When there's too much on your plate and you start stressing out about how you'll get it all done, that can bring your momentum to a screeching halt. You can also get overwhelmed just by not knowing what to do. You might be dealing with several problems at once, none of which have obvious solutions, and suddenly leaning in seems impossible because you're so consumed by the effort of coping with whatever issues have come up. Or maybe you're facing too many options and choices, or you feel like you don't have enough information to make a decision, or that all decisions will lead to bad outcomes.

Whether you are feeling overwhelmed because you've got too much going on, or because you have too many choices, there is a solution—do a *brain dump*. You must get it all out of your head and onto a piece of paper, and then start knocking it out by taking action.

Dava was walking down Newbury Street on her way to Matsu, the women's clothing store she had owned and operated for fifteen years. From the outside, she had every appearance of a happy, successful, creative professional. Awards and national magazine features adorned her walls. Her appearance was eminently fashionable— black flats from Paris, leggings from Japan, and a vibrant Italian shawl. When she stopped for coffee, she chatted with everyone in the shop because she knew them all.

But appearances, in this case, were deceiving. The bright shawl was a failed attempt to lift her spirits. The awards on her walls were from better days. And the only reason she stopped to chat was to procrastinate and stall her return to her shop. The truth was her store was doing terribly. The racks were full of unsold merchandise. She was behind on her rent. The shop itself was in need of maintenance. Each time a potential customer walked through the door, she felt nothing but resignation and the frustration of knowing that in the end she wouldn't buy anything. Dava felt completely overwhelmed.

She'd tried separating her self-esteem from the store, money, and success, but the fear didn't disappear: the fear that no one would walk through the door. The fear that her landlord would ask for the back rent. The fear that the UPS guy would show up with packages and she wouldn't have the money to pay the COD charge. She wanted to scream: *Don't people realize that if they don't come down to Newbury Street this will lead me to close my doors for good?* When she was younger, anger motivated her, but at fifty-four it was stopping her in her tracks. It seemed as if all of a sudden her life had become very small and disappointing.

When you're truly overwhelmed, it's never because of something simple. You feel overwhelmed when you're facing a big problem with multiple arms and legs. It's like living with a big, growing dark cloud hanging over your head. There is so much for you to get done, you have fears about your ability to accomplish it all, and there is no guarantee that your effort will pay off. The less clear you are about what you need to do, the more overwhelmed you will become.

You have choices to make about what direction you will head in first. Whether it is just an impossibly long to-do list at work, or a carpool and after-school schedule that requires you to be in three places at once, or a problem as massive as the recession threatening your business, there are too many things you are juggling and no clear path forward. When you have too many choices, studies have proved over and over again that you end up feeling overwhelmed by the choices in front of you so you put off making any choice at all. Which of course just leads to you feeling even more overwhelmed. You probably know people who've never managed to break this cycle, who spend their entire lives overwhelmed because they're never clear about what they need to do, and they can't handle the number of decisions they need to make.

But while it's true that shutting down and avoiding making any decision won't help, that doesn't mean you should just start flailing away at whatever crosses your path. Turning yourself into a human tornado can cause as much damage as it can help. What you need to do is start yourself moving in the right direction first. That means taking a quick scan of the situation, noting all the options, and then starting up. My point here is twofold: Clearly you need to start taking action. If you continue to consider and contemplate and worry and agonize, you're just making things worse. But to get there, you need to be smart. **If you're already in an overwhelmed state of mind, your brain is not working with all cylinders. To just "start doing something" without a moment's reflection will usually mean doing something rash and impulsive that makes you feel better, but is just one more way of avoiding the core issues.** If you've got a problem at work, doing the laundry is not going to help—it's a deliberate distraction.

So yes, you want to take action. **But first, do a brain dump.** Simply put, a brain dump is when you list all the problems and decisions that are bugging you. Break it all down. Empty out your head completely. Don't worry about what comes out. If you're doing it right, it will be a huge, random list, with everything from things to pick up at the grocery store, to issues at work, to more existential worries. There will be fears, action items, things you forgot—you'll be shocked what pours out when you just open the valve and let it drain. But that's exactly what you want. One reason you are overwhelmed is because your brain can hold only so much. You have reached maximum capacity, and it's keeping you from thinking straight. You can't manage all that stuff in your mind. That's why you keep dropping the ball and feeling so overwhelmed. Like the saying goes, you need to empty your cup so you can fill it again.

You need to dump your brain so you can use it. Once you've done this, start in on your list, doing whatever needs to get done. One at a time, begin crossing things off the Brain Dump List.

Discover a *More Powerful You*

ONE of my favorite exercises is closing my eyes and visualizing a sponge being squeezed and all the water dripping out. Now picture your brain as a giant sponge and mentally wring it out. Let it all just pour out. You can actually feel your mind physically contract and ease up. It's a very powerful exercise to use when you feel your worry and fears taking a grip on your mind. Then of course dump it all out on a piece of paper.

Dava was worried about how to keep her store open, how to pay off her outstanding bills and still have money in the bank to pay for the goods coming in for the new season. She was overwhelmed with the problem and unsure how to proceed. Her brain was scrambled. By making a list and putting down all the fears, choices, options, and decisions she had to make, she realized that she didn't need to decide them all at once. She just needed to start knocking things off the list. She moved out of her "either/or" world, and into "both/and." She didn't need to decide whether she should have a sale, update her website, take out an advertisement, write a letter to her land-lord, cancel orders for goods, or focus on inventory. By emptying her head on a piece of paper, she now had a clear mind and could move forward.

And in the process she learned an important lesson about resistance: It loves all kinds of thinking and reflecting and analysis and hand-wringing about what to do next. But as soon as she broke out of its spell, by dumping it on a piece of paper, she was in motion, and feeling much more in control of her destiny.

Half the anxiety you feel when you're overwhelmed is because you're not doing anything about it. You worry about

BRAIN DUMP

GROCERIES

1. Email $ from lululemon
2. Reseph - payment
3. Lunch program - kendall needs relief
4. oil/propane - set up auto delivery
5. Grams iphoto book
6. Premier Dance - send email
7. Book blog - upload Sabe
8. Refund $$ $ from event
9. Meeting for Margaret
10. Cancel
11. Check to Openfields
12. Sawyer - summer camp research
13. Oak. who's little league sign up?
14. Amigo - needs rabies shot
15. Kendall passport before trip next month
16. Set up bill pay for cc#s
17. Jill @ Hudson return call
18. When's next Success Magazine article due?
19. Election - need motion light installed over garage.
20. Call Amy Johnson about Spalt Hawk dates
21. Follow up w J Holwoon RE: corp sig.
22. Talk to Connie RE: new banner for blog
23. Send MOM - FREEDOM

1. cream cheese
2. miracle whip
3. marange
4. yogurts
5. lunch meat
6. bananas
7. lettuce
8. cucumbers.

*remember to return the Non HE ~~detergent~~ Laundry detergent

24. Chris bday present.
25. Sawyer Lab clinic
26. Mtg w Dawn
27. Cancel dentist Wed.
28. Record books

promos
29. Call Jodi
30. New Year Cards get ordered!
31. Donate old kids outerwear. get to bonder piles!
32. Follow up w GE on washing machine
33. Program XBOX
34. Transfer iTunes library to computer →

choices and outcomes as if your life is falling apart before your eyes. But something happens the moment you stop worrying and start doing. **Action removes doubt. The moment you take stock of the situation and start actually doing something about it, you begin to feel better. You feel a sense of control returning to you.** By confronting the difficult decisions with action, you are asserting ownership over your life, instead of allowing it to be directed by outside forces.

Another thing Dava learned when she started taking steps to increasing the business in her boutique is that all the tension around finding the "right" decision quickly faded. In a world of choices, it often comes down to *how* we make choices, not *what* choices we make. When you get overwhelmed you approach every decision as if it is superserious and carries massive risk. But most of the time, there is no wrong choice. Even the biggest decisions can be shifted or reconsidered with a little time and effort. For a long time, Dava considered every single decision as if it had life-or-death consequences. When she saw the UPS truck pull up in front of the store, she had a panic attack because her mind started to list off the parade of horrible outcomes: *I don't have the money to write the check for these goods. If I don't get new goods into the store, I won't have fresh merchandise to sell this fall. If I don't have fresh merchandise my customers won't be inspired to come back. If they don't start coming, I am out of business, and so on, and so on.*

But once she started knocking things off her list, Dava realized that the power and energy that took her out of her slump could easily be redirected to the next challenge. When the UPS truck arrived she had the confidence and the clarity to take control. She told him to wait right there, called her vendor, and asked if she could postdate the check sixty days. If not she had to return the goods. Because of the brain dump, her mind was clear and she could be creative and find solutions instead of just panicking. "I just realized that even if the worst happened, even if I had to close the store," she said, "I would always have options, as long as I was willing to make it work."

She understood that even if she made the wrong choice, it didn't matter because she could fight her way through the consequences. In other words, she could let go of that overwhelmed feeling, because the decision was much less important than her momentum.

A fear of making big decisions is rooted in the belief that you will get locked in. The simple fact is that your powerful self can shift the direction of anything. You can start out accepting a job offer, and discover within three months that it's the wrong path. Maybe you moved your whole family and relocated. There's nothing in this situation that definitively means you messed up. In fact, it could be the perfect opportunity to reinvent your job. Instead of leaping into the next thing, what if you hunkered down and created a change from within the organization?

The key is to divide and conquer. If you've gotten yourself into a tight squeeze and you don't know how to make your next move, write down all your options. Break it down to a level where you can start listing things that you could do today. Now just pick one and get it done. Power through it, even if it's not the most important piece. The key is that you're taking action. The simple act of doing is its own form of energy. You don't need to ponder the best choice, you just need to do something now.

Focus on the feeling you get as you power through. Consider how it feels to cross something real off your list. Compare it to how you felt before. Now what's next?

As soon as the showroom calls back, the UPS truck arrives, or the price for a booth at the trade show is three times what she thought it would be, Dava feels a pang of panic. But the most important part is she has taken one step closer to getting what she wants. The more she does it, the easier it will get to defeat the feeling. A year later, a daily brain dump is part of her daily return and her business has benefited. Not only is her store, Matsu, thriving but so is her new jewelry line NYMPH and her new perfume and candle line. When you empty your head you become more effective and capable of taking on even more!

Dealing with a Lack of Motivation

When you start to feel unmotivated, you will look for ways to weasel out of your commitments. We all do it. If there's a stealth way to back out, without ever losing face, you will do it without hesitation. That's why, the second you start to feel your motivation slipping, you need to arrange a consequence for inaction and leave yourself no choice but to continue to push through.

If you see yourself losing your edge, or allowing yourself to start to let your deadlines slide, or if you feel distracted or unfocused— a lack of motivation is kicking in. This feeling comes from being disconnected with your own actions, which kicks off a vicious cycle of becoming even less motivated, which leads to taking less action. In other words, you don't feel motivated because you're not doing anything, and then you don't do anything because you're not motivated. If you're putting off action and waiting to feel motivated, you're never going to do anything, because motivation comes from taking action. If you want to maintain your momentum, you need to remain vigilant against any kind of delay. Just like weeding a garden, you always need to be on the lookout for thoughts that would push you to delay.

Putting off a decision or an action for any number of apparently valid reasons should be viewed with extreme prejudice. Remember that your brain is an excuse machine. Your brain's natural love for stories comes with a plausibility bias. If the excuse you've invented sounds halfway plausible, you'll buy it, especially when it means getting out of doing something that feels risky. Delaying is one of the primary tools resistance uses to keep you stuck. In truth there are very few things that ever need to wait. Even if you're waiting on one thing, there's no reason that you can't be moving forward on another front.

A close variant is analysis and rationalization. If you're ruminating over your next move, or turning an idea over too much, you're stuck. There's no reason for you to be sitting around and overthinking. In most cases, this is just the expression of a conceit of your conscious mind. It's the "lemme think about it" bias. The truth is that when you're sitting and turning an idea around in your mind, you've already got the problem worked out in your unconscious mind. Those additional days you tack on are just the expression of your mind's desire to avoid the decision altogether.

Now there's nothing quite like a good night's sleep to allow you to fully absorb an idea. But there's a huge difference between deciding something in the morning, and putting off the decision for a few days. In the former case, you're allowing your mind to fully process the idea—you're turning the idea over to your automatic unconscious processes and allowing them to fully examine it. In the latter case, you're just feeding your resistance.

Doing something—dismantling the fears by taking them apart and steamrolling through them—is the only form of being powerful. Thinking is just hot air. If you really want to take the time to mull over an idea, try doing something else at the same time—maybe do some exercise while you're at it. Nor should you feel afraid to just release the idea to all those machines humming in the back of your mind and see what they say. Your automatic unconscious processes don't need much time to come to a decision, and they are usually spot on.

If you're saying to yourself that something just "is what it is," then you're allowing yourself to become stuck. There's absolutely no reason that you can't exert a huge influence over *every* area of your life. When you've committed to a direction, you just need to swarm that path. That means that you need to attack from multiple angles.

Think about what a brilliant strategy Seth used to force himself out of that plane. He forced himself to jump because he put himself in a position where he could not weasel out of it even if he wanted to. It was already too late. He was up in the air, the door was open, and he was strapped to some guy who was getting paid to jump out that door whether Seth was leading the way or being dragged out kicking and screaming.

Lauren Zander, the woman who trained me to be a coach, once told me how she gets people to quit smoking cigarettes or lose weight: Every time you light up a cigarette or cheat on a diet, you must throw twenty dollars out the window. Research has since proven that when you put yourself on the line with others and create a penalty for not sticking to a promise you've made with yourself, you will be far more likely to keep your promise. This is the power of others. They keep you accountable. Lauren was taking it even a step further—she didn't want you to give the twenty dollars to someone else or a charity because you could rationalize that it would be put to good use. Throwing a perfectly good twenty-dollar bill out the window of a moving car or tossing it into a public trash can just makes you want to scream, and crucially, not light up again.

Dan Ariely, a professor of behavioral economics from Duke University, covers this idea in depth. Based on his experiments with adults and students in all sorts of settings, he has found that committing to goals with hard and clear deadlines, and then informing your friends, spouses, or work colleagues about them, has a very beneficial effect on outcomes. You will be much more likely to meet your goal by making a clear and public commitment.

So if you want to stop feeling powerless and alone, start thinking about a change that you want to make, and start talking about it. Get out and discuss it with anyone who will listen. Tell that person that you want her to check in with you. Make yourself accountable to her. And if you really want to make it stick, put some money down, or better yet, throw it out a window. Tell her that you'll pay a penalty if you don't follow through. There's nothing like the prospect of a loss to motivate you and get you out of a funk.

Arranging a consequence for inaction to overcome a lack of motivation comes down to a simple concept: Your brain will do anything it can to avoid perceived danger or risk. Most of the time, it will always perceive more danger in taking action than in not taking action, which is why it tries to keep you stuck. You can overcome this by arranging things so that there is a negative consequence to *not* taking action. It doesn't have to be something horrible, it just has to be a consequence that your brain won't want. If Seth had tried to back out of skydiving at the last minute, he would have had to deal with the embarrassment of acting like a scaredy-cat in front of the instructor, and he would have wasted a good amount of money. His brain didn't want that, which meant that backing out no longer seemed like the safe choice. He outsmarted his own resistance.

Discover a *More Powerful You*

THERE are lots of ways you can arrange a consequence for inaction to ward off a lack of motivation. Take exercise for example. If you keep finding ways to blow it off, convince a friend to exercise with you and then ask him or her to meet at your house to start the walk, or pick you up on the way to the gym. If someone is standing in your kitchen ready to go, or if you hear the horn honking in the driveway signaling that your ride is ready, you won't be weaseling out of it.

1. How do you avoid your commitment to change?
2. How could you use someone else to penalize you to force yourself to do it?
3. Who is that person?
4. What could you do to leave yourself no choice?
5. Is there a class, workshop, training, or seminar that you've been putting off committing to doing because you are too busy? Just sign up. Pay in full. You have five seconds—go do it.

Dealing with Feeling Like You're a Fraud

Everyone knows what feeling like a fraud is like. You're trying your best, and things might even be going well on the surface, but inside you're a mess. You're trying to act confident in your new business, but truthfully you feel as if you have no clue what you're doing. You've been going to the gym and dieting, but you still feel fat and as if you don't even belong on that treadmill. It happens to all of us, no matter how accomplished or successful we become.

The moment you start feeling like a fraud, you need to reconnect with some of your most positive and successful friends and let them know that you are having a hard time aligning your confidence level with your goals. Every one of us has felt that before. It's one of the growing pains of getting what you want. It's not a sign that you're a failure, in fact it's the opposite. The more successful you become, the more experiences you'll have where your feelings about yourself and your abilities don't match what you're trying to accomplish.

Connecting with people lets you draft off their own personal momentum a little. All sorts of experiments show that social networks are actually agents that transfer behaviors. That means the people you hang out with and socialize with will have a significant influence on just how you feel and behave. So just by talking to the three most motivated, successful, and goal-oriented friends you have, their momentum will actually rub off and influence your behavior. And since they're successful, they'll understand exactly where you're coming from when you describe feeling like a fraud, which will help remind you that everyone feels that way sometimes.

A second advantage to getting out there and talking with people about your goals and setbacks is that even just discussing your efforts can help build momentum. Even if you have not completely accomplished your goal, the mere fact that you're in the process of trying to make it work is impressive to other people—and even to yourself. Once you have the chance to start publicly describing your own story and your trials and tribulations, you begin creating a personal success narrative that you can hang onto. If you're at the gym thinking "What is a fatso like me doing here? I don't belong here with all these fit, athletic people," that's discouraging. But if you're describing how you feel to someone else and say, "I just feel so out of shape, like I don't even belong at the gym, but I force myself to go anyway," then suddenly it doesn't sound so bad. In fact, it sounds admirable and impressive. By talking about your negative feelings within the context of trying to accomplish your goals, you incorporate them into your own triumphant narrative.

Having a positive personal narrative is a crucial component of building personal power. The actual facts of your situation are much less important than the story you tell yourself. Even if the narrative you create isn't quite real, just talking about it starts to make it real. It becomes a dress rehearsal for your real success. In fact, a growing body of experimental evidence shows how a critical part of mental health consists of using illusions about your own level of control over your destiny. While psychologists have spent decades trying to help people ground their thoughts in reality, it turns out that some of the healthiest and happiest people have a substantially exaggerated belief in both their ability to control their situation and that some higher purpose guided them. It's called the "illusion of control."

It's no accident that it works. Storing up a belief in your own powers is what pushes you forward toward future goals and helps drive your momentum. It's a healthy revisionism that's willing to bend the facts a little in order to create a narrative of success. When you start talking about yourself, and start building a story that connects a series of small successes, you start feeling better about yourself, and that gives you the power to start moving forward. Your story is a way of building up bragging rights, which helps you feel better about taking on the next challenge.

The Power of *Self-Deception*

ONE night in a booth in the back of Philadelphia's famous Smokey Joe's bar, two drunken professors from the University of Pennsylvania wrote an experiment on a napkin, and tipped the world of psychology on its head. They had a hunch about what really makes people happy and successful, and wanted to prove it. Like giggling schoolboys, they thought up the most outrageous questions they could imagine. The kind of questions that everyone would rather avoid answering: "Do you enjoy your bowel movements?," "Do you ever doubt your sexual adequacy?," "Have you ever wanted to rape or be raped by someone?"

A few weeks later, after persuading the ethics panel that they had a scientific mission beyond just humiliating undergraduates with embarrassing questions, they tested out their theory on a group of students.

Their famous Self-Deception Questionnaire measured your ability to fool yourself. Assuming you answer the questions with absolute honesty, you reveal your innate ability to keep certain ugly truths about yourself at bay—because you may not want to *admit* that you enjoy a bowel movement, but among academics and psychologists, it's an accepted truth that everyone actually does. The more your mind refuses to accept these universal truths, the more you're demonstrating an ability to unconsciously and automatically warp the facts about your own inner feelings. You can literally fool yourself, while deep down knowing the real truth.

What really rocked everyone about the results was discovering that these so-called self-deceivers were not pathological or mentally suspect. In fact, our drunken professors, Gur and Sackeim, had discovered that the ability to deceive ourselves is not merely a central part of our mental processes, but actually a fundamental ingredient in our success and happiness. In experiments that followed, the people who "failed" the Self-Deception Questionnaire and lied best to themselves proved to be the ones who were happiest, most successful, and well adjusted among any crowd.

It makes sense. The shrinks might call them self-deceivers, but these people are really just blockers. They have mastered the mental judo of keeping harmful information out of their brains. They don't ruminate over depressing facts and fears. They don't worry about what's wrong with them, or all the reasons *why not.*

That's not to say they're unrealistic or living in total denial. These are people who simply have a natural knack for keeping their egos inflated. They focus on the positive. Their brain machines have found a way to keep stressful information out, which lets them perform better.

Dealing with Feeling Discouraged

When you are building your personal power, you are walking a line between pushing yourself past your resistance and pushing yourself too hard into a ditch. You need to be constantly aware of how you feel, and balancing resistance against genuine pain. If there's no pleasure in your breakthroughs, because they completely empty you out, you've got to lower the voltage.

Inevitably, those kind of overly radical changes are going to require some high-intensity work. If it's too radical, you can actually lose momentum.

Remember how Ellen felt the first time she went to the yoga class? That first class gave her a sense that she could break through in her weight loss. That lasted for a little while, but to really convert that success into true momentum, she needed to get some pleasure out of the exercise. She needed to start feeling good. And she did. But that meant not getting into a death-grip focus on how well she was doing during class. Instead, she just focused on showing up. That was it. Showing up was hard enough, but she discovered something. By staying present to the moment and not trying to wrestle her resistance to the ground in one fell swoop, she started finding parts of the whole experience that she enjoyed. She found that if she backed off on the really tough positions, and took a few rests, that she could survive a class and not feel completely destroyed afterward. She actually felt better, too. All that sweating made her feel extremely refreshed, and her skin started glowing in a way that people really noticed. They asked her if she'd gone skiing over the weekend, because she looked like she'd gotten some sun. Even though she hadn't lost as much weight as she hoped, and even though she could hardly bend over in a correct "down dog," she felt better than ever.

That's the key to being powerful. Improvising to fit the situation. Building on each little victory, to take you to the next. Ellen went from the thrill of discovering that she could survive a yoga class, to the pride of being able to stick with it, to the physical pleasure of feeling revitalized. She sustained momentum by knowing instinctively where to apply pressure, and where to let pressure off, while still sticking to the greater goals. Momentum came from living in the present and honoring her efforts, while constantly ignoring her resistance.

Monica hasn't been as successful in building momentum and becoming more powerful. She's been working as a financial analyst for most of her adult life. She's very good at it, and she's managed to parlay her talent into a decent arrangement. She works part-time for a large company, managing its budget, and she telecommutes most days. She's got an extremely flexible schedule that lets her be with her three kids after school. She sometimes wonders, though, whether she's trapped in a "golden cage," since anything but this job will be a step down in flexibility and pay. Secretly, she holds onto a dream of opening a small design boutique, featuring a mix of local artists and imported crafts. Her house contains small prototypes of various pieces of glasswork and furniture she's commissioned from friends, or brought back from exotic trips, as potential pieces for the shop. She tells anyone who listens that, "I've been doing this same financial thing for fifteen years, but I want to do something besides working on spreadsheets. I want to be more social."

Money is a big obstacle to her moving forward right now. She and her husband make enough to live comfortably, but there's not much left over to play with, let alone to make a substantial investment in her idea. She doesn't want to put the family finances in jeopardy. She feels that it's got to be done in phases. First, trunk shows that lead to temporary stores over holidays, and then a real store. She's absolutely right about that approach.

So why isn't she gaining speed on the idea? Because there's always something else going on. Kids, laundry, groceries, and a day job. You deal with all of that and you feel like you need a break at night. Plus, there's no crisis giving urgency to her dream. As she told me recently, "I feel busy enough with the job and the kids' schedule. It also feels a little scary, doing the necessary traveling and finding the things I'd need to make the store work. The flights to foreign countries, the negotiations, and all that. But the truth is that I have the perfect skills for it. It's kind of insane not to do it."

It's happening for Monica, but at a snail's pace. She makes a point of meeting someone new every month or so—a lawyer, a local businessperson. With each step she gets really excited, but then her momentum fades. Monica's only problem is the pace at which she is working on her idea. She works in bursts of intense activity, once a month or so. That will burn out any idea or pursuit. Changing your life is a race of distance, not speed. You need stamina to maintain your momentum.

A great rule of thumb is that frequency is more important than intensity or quantity. The number of days or hours in a row that you commit to a change is a much better indicator of your true momentum than the number of miles you run in a few desperate spurts, or the number of pages you read, or the number of calls you make. If Monica were to spend just twenty minutes a day on her idea she'd be better programmed for success.

Another trick you can use is focusing on how you'll feel when you're done. **Thinking about getting out of bed on a cold rainy morning isn't enticing at all. But picturing yourself in that hot shower after a fantastic workout will lure you out of bed.** That's because you're trying to fight a positive emotion—for example, the immediate sensation of comfort under the covers and the darkness and the chill morning air outside of them—with an abstract, intellectual argument about the virtues of physical fitness won't work. But on the other hand, if you decide to push through your resistance by thinking about how great you'll feel when you've finished jogging, that's something your brain can hang onto.

But this only works if you actually feel good when you're done. You need to feel pleasure when it's over, and you need to be physically and mentally present when it happens. You need to be there when you have a breakthrough. If you're heaving by the side of the road instead of enjoying the sound of the morning birds, or you can barely walk because your legs are so tired instead of feeling revitalized, or you're sick from staying up too many nights in a row instead of feeling that tired satisfaction of a good evening's work, you're pushing yourself too hard. Your mental determination to push through is overpowering your capacity to enjoy the genuine pleasure of a breakthrough.

The best way to be there right now, in the present, is when your resistance is not wailing like an air-raid siren. It's when you've pushed past the first bit of inertia and settled into a true groove.

Enjoy it! You deserve a little pleasure from the experience. Monica needs to structure her daily twenty minutes as if it's a treat—like online shopping or flipping through a fashion magazine. As if it's a small reward she is looking forward to getting to after a long tiring day. Becoming powerful is not punishment—it's the discovery of something more past your resistance. If that means giving yourself a few extra days to hit the target, then give yourself that small amount of slack—whatever it's going to take to let you stay with it. The point of pushing through is to teach yourself the reason for doing it again and again, not frighten you away further.

That might mean dropping the jog to a brisk walk, so you can keep luring yourself out there with the splendor of a fresh start every morning. That might mean allowing yourself a little more time to come up with your business plan, so you have time to let the creative process unfold.

Notice I didn't say cut down the number of morning jogs—just the speed and the mileage. Notice I didn't say take a few nights off when you're drawing up that business plan. Notice I didn't say reward yourself just because you did something supposedly "difficult." I'm not talking about training yourself like some sort of puppy dog. You cannot let down your guard to the real dangers of inertia.

CHAPTER ELEVEN

The Seven-Day Stamina Challenge

If you really want to change your life, and you want to pick up the pace of change, then there's one thing you must do. You must exercise for a minimum of twenty minutes *every day*.

I cannot overstate how important is it for you to exercise if you want to bring momentum into your life. The biochemical cocktail that you release into your body every time you push your muscles and your heart to work a little harder is like a momentum potion.

A simple twenty-minute workout at your target heart rate unleashes what Dr. John Ratey at the Harvard Medical School has called "Miracle-Gro for the brain." The effects are astounding. Not only does it clear your mind, but it increases speed of processing, stimulates the growth of memory cells, and primes your brain for its best learning for ninety minutes after you exercise. Anything you do in those ninety minutes you will execute with more precision, focus, and speed than before. In a landmark fifteen-year-long study, Dr. Ratey has documented the effects of twenty minutes of exercise at the Naperville school system in Illinois.

After agreeing to participate in the study, this school's students don't simply play dodgeball and soccer. They wear a heart rate monitor and are graded on the amount of time they are able to keep their heart rate in the optimal aerobic range for their body type. After PE the kids attend classes like normal.

Once the students started focusing on physical activity at a target heart rate, the test scores of the entire student body jumped. In math they placed sixth in the world. On the science section Naperville shocked everyone when they outscored every other school in the world. Think about it. Naperville became the number-one high school in science in the world, not by studying more science, but by exercising.

If you want to think clearer, beat stress, put the damper on your depression, boost your confidence, and get unstuck, you simply need to exercise. If you've always thought of exercise as just something you "had to" or were "supposed to" do—think again. If you are exercising just to keep your butt smaller than its genetic predisposition, there's an even better reason than vanity.

Exercise is truly a secret weapon, a way of priming your mind for success. When you're stuck and can't figure something out, and you're looking for an excuse to run away from a problem— go for it! Just stay within your target heart rate. Because when you're running or exercising, you're actually clearing your mind of all the garbage and resistance that's gumming it up.

You're going to feel sharper and more focused than ever. And of course it makes sense. You're pushing through, simply on a different front. No one really wants to exercise. The first three minutes of a workout can be difficult. If you're out of shape, the first three weeks of working out can be tough. I know you're busy. You're stressed out. There just isn't time. But exercising is not an optional activity if you're trying to gain momentum. Pushing through and exercising is how you get momentum, build stamina, and increase the pace of change in your life.

The Seven-Day Stamina Workout

Stamina to push through your fears and frustrations is something you can build in a very meaningful low-risk way. The more you exercise the muscle to push through your fears and frustrations, the easier it will become. I've combined this idea with a decade's worth of research on happiness to come up with a seven-day program that will boost your stamina for making changes in your life and also increase your happiness at the same time.

In the last decade there has been an explosion of research conducted on happiness. Scientists can tell you that once you reach seventy-five thousand dollars a year in annual income, your happiness won't rise much more based on money, and you'll need to find other ways to become a happier person. Psychologists and business gurus unilaterally agree that being a glass-half-full, positive person affects your life in immeasurable ways and makes you much more successful in business. It is an advantage to cultivate happiness and a positive mind-set, no doubt. Based on several key studies, the factors that raise happiness are undisputed and obvious in their simplicity: spending time with close friends and loved ones, home-cooked meals/family dinners, a night out with friends, exercising regularly, a fun trip that you are anticipating and planning, a good night's sleep, a positive outlook, and meaningful work. Happiness isn't rocket science—far from it. But just like learning to take action, you do have to work at it. Life is so busy, it's the simple and obvious things that you tend to drop by the wayside.

Consider this seven-day program a chance to teach yourself to become an expert at taking action and boost your level of overall happiness along the way. All you have to do is follow the rules and you'll understand very quickly why taking action on the simplest things is so bloody hard. Every day, you will add a new action that will help you build the skills you need in order to change your life. And the actions you take relate to boosting your mind-set, your momentum, and your enjoyment of life. Here's how you do it:

Day *One*

1. Face the day: The night before, set your alarm for thirty minutes earlier than you normally wake up. The next morning, as soon as the alarm sounds, open your eyes, throw off the covers, sit up and put your feet on the floor, and stand up. Your day starts now. No delay. No pillow over the head. No snooze. If you lay in bed more than ten seconds before standing up, you fail the first test. If you fail the test, start over tomorrow. Do not advance to day two until you've passed day one.

Day *Two*

1. Face the day
2. Admit it: Before you get dressed, write in a journal for five minutes. Write about the big, embarrassing idea that you want to make happen. Describe in great detail how you will feel when this happens. Describe what happened along the way. Put in some first-person details—describe what you see as you are in the scene itself. Don't think about what to write. Just write. No one will be reading it but you. Do a brain dump and flush out your obstacle thinking on the paper and brainstorm ways to work around each issue you see. Write down one action you will take today to move

yourself closer. Schedule the time you will do it into your calendar. If you fail to "Face the day" or fail to write in your journal, or you don't take the action you promised to take, you fail the test. Do not advance to day three until you pass day two.

Day *Three*

1. Face the day

2. Admit it

3. Exercise twenty minutes: You know the benefits of exercise. You know that getting outside increases your happiness. Regardless of the weather and how tired you feel and how much you don't want to, head out for twenty minutes before breakfast and take a brisk walk or a run. And don't even think about complaining about not having the time. You set your alarm for thirty minutes earlier than you normally wake up in "face the day." Between the five minutes it takes to write in the journal, and the five minutes to change into your exercise gear, that leaves twenty minutes to get outside for the brisk walk or run. If you need to buy more time, get up earlier or sleep in your exercise clothes. You'd be shocked how much just having the clothes on your body when you get out of bed will push you to exercise. If you fail to "face the day," "admit it," or fail to do twenty minutes of exercise, do not go to day four.

Day *Four*

1. Face the day

2. Admit it

3. Exercise twenty minutes

4. Break your routine: Drive a new way to work. Stop at a

different place for coffee than your normal spot. Lock your cell
phone in the trunk of the car while you drive. Listen to a different
station the whole way in; don't change the station on the commercial
break. Order something totally off the wall for lunch. Brush your
teeth with your left hand. Borrow your roommate's or your kids'
iPod and run to someone else's playlist. In a small but meaningful
way, find a way to break from your daily routine. If you fail to do it,
do not go to day five until you pass day four.

Day *Five*

1. **Face the day**
2. **Admit it**
3. **Exercise twenty minutes**
4. **Break your routine**
5. **Make eye contact:** Make eye contact with five strangers today.
Stare at them until they look back at you. Then smile in a friendly
easy smile and hold your gaze. Count to four. One. Two. Three.
Four. If you fail to do this with five strangers, you fail. Do not move
on to day six, until you pass day five.

Day *Six*

1. **Face the Day**
2. **Admit it**
3. **Exercise twenty minutes**
4. **Break your routine**
5. **Make eye contact**
6. **Go public:** Meet or speak with two people about your big,
embarrassing idea and ask for advice. One is someone you know,
the other is a total stranger. "Excuse me, can I ask you for some

advice . . ." If you fail to have these two conversations, you fail the day. Do not move on to day seven, until you pass day six.

Day *Seven*

1. **Face the day**
2. **Admit it**
3. **Exercise twenty minutes**
4. **Break your routine**
5. **Make eye contact**
6. **Go public**
7. **Connect:** Plan and cook dinner for someone you love. When you sit down for dinner, don't talk about yourself—ask this person about his or her life. Be interested and use your interest as a guide to make the conversation flow.

The beauty of this stamina workout is that it helps you practice building stamina in the areas of your life that have the greatest impact on your success, your health, and your happiness. Every one of these challenges will help you push closer to what you want in life. Every one will deliver the one-two punch of feeling dread or fear and then the rush of control once you take action. If you can complete this seven-day stamina workout, you will be on your way to becoming an expert at taking action.

More important, you will be building into your life a daily routine that forces you to get up on time, focus your mind on your dreams so that you are primed to spot them, exercise and reap the mental benefits of Miracle-Gro for the brain, seek advice and support about your dreams, and connect with someone you love over a home-cooked meal. If you managed to do those things every day, your life would be unrecognizable in six months.

After all that you've learned, you now know that pushing through fear and frustration in any moment is a choice. In the past, you chose to stay overwhelmed. You remained uncertain. You allowed yourself to be paralyzed. You now have a different path to choose. Of course you can have whatever you want and your life can be so much larger than it is. You can answer that calling. Whether or not you do is a choice you have to make.

One of the most widely read books of all time, *The Alchemist* carried this same simple message. As the shepherd Santiago abandons his flock of sheep and travels halfway around the world in search of treasure and his personal legend, he hits many obstacles, setbacks, and struggles. And at each twist and turn in the road, at each setback he felt or wall he hit "he realized that he had to choose between thinking of himself as a poor victim of a thief and as an adventurer in a quest for his treasure."

What will you choose? Will you be a victim of circumstance, or an adventurer on a quest to fulfill your dreams?

So What Do You Want to Do
with Your Life, Anyhow?

Now that you've got a little taste for how the world conspires to keep us stuck, and how you can shake loose from it to get what you want, it's time to zoom out and consider what this means about the experience of life. When you look at the most philosophical aspect of being stuck, there are really two basic concepts that cut to the heart of it. These are struggles that occupy everyone throughout his or her life. As Reverend Peter Gomes, the Harvard theologian, said that morning, the quest is the same for us all: "to become who you were meant to be." We all know there's something so much larger intended for our lives and we struggle to figure out what it is and how to find it. But when you're stuck, you've engineered a way to avoid these struggles.

These two struggles are **ownership** and **challenge**. In the first case, when you're stuck, you're dancing around the question of your personal responsibility for the direction of your life. You're fudging that line between what you can't control and what you can. In the second case, when you're stuck, you're refusing to push yourself into situations that will test your abilities. By avoiding the challenge, you avoid change.

Do You Own Your Life? Or Are You Just Playing by Someone Else's Rules?

Underlying all feelings of being stuck is a basic problem with ownership. If you don't own, or accept, the everyday occurrences in your day, you will begin to feel a distance from your own life. Whatever degree you feel like the things that happen to you are outside your control, that's exactly how much you're going to feel like a stranger in your life. Let's trace the origins of that feeling and all the secondary problems it creates.

A feeling of control is essential to your mental health. If you start feeling as if you're not in the driver's seat, and the conditions of your life cannot be controlled by your own actions, when things go wrong you quickly start to enter into a negative spiral known as *learned helplessness*. Psychologists have reproduced this condition in lab animals and humans by subjecting them to stress that they can't seem to control. Under those conditions, people and animals quickly give up trying to fight. They accept not merely the fact that they can't stop the stress that those nasty scientists are inflicting, but they actually start to assume that they can't control a whole slew of additional circumstances. They withdraw ownership of their situation.

You don't need electric shocks and cages to make people give up trying. A classic experiment can be reproduced in any classroom setting. You hand out a test to every member of a classroom. Everyone believes it's the same test, but you secretly give half the class a sequence of four fairly simple word jumble problems (try to unscramble *nopso, korf, efink, altep*), and the other half a list of three words that are impossible to unscramble, but the final word being exactly like the other group (try to unscramble *horthes, kinrok, medrub, altep*). You ask each student to solve the first problem, and tell him to raise his hand when he's done. Sure enough, half the hands go up quickly, while the other half struggles in vain. You repeat the same exercise for the remaining words quickly in succession, so the students don't get the chance to figure out what's different about their lists. As you're going, you might observe something happen in the faces of the students with the impossible words. They start to worry that they are total idiots. You've activated a core doubt in their minds. By the time they reach the fourth word—which everyone should easily solve—most of the unlucky group will be helplessly stuck. The intimidation, embarrassment, and frustration of watching other students solve apparently impossible problems just zaps their brain. Their minds actually freeze, and they become unable to unscramble a word they might have easily cracked any other day.

From banging our heads against any sort of bureaucratic, academic, professional, or relational wall, many of us have acquired some amount of learned helplessness in our lives. If the words, "Why bother," or "It is what it is," or "It's not so bad," have ever escaped your mouth, you've felt some form of learned helplessness. Maybe you got tired of feeling like your own actions don't add up. Maybe you set yourself up for failure by shooting for an oversize goal and trying to do more than you could—and when you felt the disappointment and consequences, you gave up trying for anything else.

Regardless of where you built that wall inside your mind, the point is that you retreated from ownership of the problem. You adopted helplessness as a strategy, in the face of losing odds, and accepted an inability to change things. You convinced yourself that it's not worth the effort.

When you allow this kind of thinking to install itself in your life, and you retreat further and further from areas that you feel you "can't control," you settle into a vicious cycle. A sense of discouragement settles into your life, and you're locked into smaller, more ineffectual methods to soothe that pain. You end up focusing on the little that you feel you can control, and avoiding the deeper, underlying problems.

Classic signs of retreat are found in the stories you tell yourself. You build stories in your mind that let you push away the blame. You focus on the details that were clearly outside your control, and gloss over the ways you might have influenced the situation. You anchor the situation around the fixed circumstances and all the specific details that kept it out of your hands. The clever trick in all these stories and brain propaganda is that there's always a kernel of truth—obviously there's going to be parts of any situation outside your control. But why is it that in these personal narratives, you never ask yourself the tough questions—*Why didn't I say something? Why didn't I express what I wanted?*

Ownership of your life cuts straight to your own vision of the future. If you don't assume control over major portions of your life, you're going to feel like a passenger. You'll have nothing to look forward to, except what life hands you. That's why you need to inhabit your life as if you own it. Owning your decisions, owning parts of your life even when they're difficult, is what allows you to create a life and make it your own. "Personalize" it.

Jerry Seinfeld has a hilarious routine where he talks about the calm distance that everyone takes when stepping into the backseat of a New York City taxicab. From behind the glass partition, we watch like television spectators as the driver takes our life into his hands, weaving between lanes at high speeds. "Wow, that looked dangerous. I don't think I'd try that in my car."

Ownership of our lives doesn't just apply to stressful situations. Most of us are actually very happy to relinquish control of even the easier parts of our lives to something else. For lots of things it makes sense. It takes away a lot of pressure and offloads work we don't care to tackle. I'm quite happy to visit an accountant every year so he can figure out my taxes for me. My husband is only too willing to let some college kids mow the lawn. But in a service-oriented society, where you can outsource everything from dog walking to personal shopping, there's a line we cross when we give away too much of our personal lives. And we never realize it's happened until it's too late.

Reasserting ownership over your life is essential. As you work at building a stronger connection between your deepest dreams and your daily actions, you'll start to focus on feeling control during specific moments when you take action. As you stack up a series of small successes, it will add up to a larger sense of control.

For now, you simply need to start thinking about the ways you've relinquished ownership of your life—both the good parts and the bad. That doesn't necessarily mean that you need to start doing your taxes and mowing the lawn. But you do need to start figuring out how to reestablish a real connection with your daily life. Are you making dinner at night, or relying on takeout? Are you watching whatever some television executive decides to stick in front of you, or have you decided to watch every movie of Hitchcock's complete works? Are you rolling up your sleeves, digging into the soil of your daily life, and building a personal connection with the events of your day? Sometimes those mindless chores, and all that dirt under your fingernails, can be an important reminder that you are in control. Without those reminders, you're still sitting behind that taxicab's glass partition.

Are You Doing Something That You Think Is Cool?

A second core component of getting stuck, closely entwined with ownership, is the problem of challenge. In a world based on convenience and choice, where saving time and the ability to weigh your options are the ultimate currency, "easy" can actually strip the joy from your life.

Everyone knows that challenges lead to growth. Our parents taught us that. But knowing and doing are very different. You might know that it's better to take the stairs, but when was the last time you skipped an elevator ride? You might know that learning is a lifetime challenge, but when was the last time you really tried to study something completely new?

Like everyone else, when you reached adulthood, you discovered that you had acquired some real freedom. You could do what you wanted, and no one was going to give you a hard time. You didn't have to make your bed every morning, you could stay up all night, you could drink beer before noon—whatever. Sure you had to fulfill some basic expectations in order to stay employed, but you had a lot more room to do what you want. At a certain level, you realized that no one was really there to boss you around anymore.

If you were like me, the dizzy realization of that kind of freedom had your head spinning for several years. I'll admit that for a while,

I was coasting. But one morning I woke up and realized that along with the freedom came the problem of actually constructing my own life. It hit me like a punch in the gut because the words "freedom is responsibility" finally took on concrete meaning. It sounds good on paper, but what it really meant to me at that moment was, "Sure, you can do whatever you want, but if you don't make anything of yourself, it's going to be your own fault."

I remembered as a kid my parents pushing me in all sorts of ways I hated. Everything from eating beets, to trying out for chorus, to calling up kids from my class and arranging my playdates. Once I grew up, no one was doing that for me anymore. No one was there to push me into uncomfortable situations and test my limits. I realized that without that push, without that voice telling me to try something new, I was going stale inside.

Many people still don't get it. They take on the trappings of adulthood and tackle fake challenges. Fake challenges are things that might be hard for other people, but come pretty easily to you—or that you've already learned how to overcome. Real challenge means doing something you don't want to do. It means pushing yourself in ways that feel uncomfortable and wrong. It means locking yourself into a situation that you may not enjoy, and discovering not simply that you've got the ability to power through it, but that you can actually thrive.

Avoiding difficult situations is not the secret bonus prize that you win by entering adulthood. Lots of people act as if it is, and it's a quiet inside joke among us all. Just because you're a grown-up doesn't mean you're off the hook. You have an embedded need to continue growing and learning. It's a personal, individual mission that requires letting go of what feels comfortable. If you choose to ignore that need, and if you refuse to face up to honest challenges, you will become stuck.

We all want to become something bigger and more powerful than we are. It's built into our DNA. That's why you're reading this book. As long as you are breathing, you will be looking for something more. What you decide to do with that feeling—stuff it or act on it—determines the direction of your life.

The longing you feel inside you is not a curse. You will always feel a tension between your current life and a longing for something more. The need for a challenge is lifelong, and there's strong research to back it up. Abraham Maslow's famous hierarchy of needs, a classic of Psych 101, perfectly explains this dynamic: All humans are driven to meet their basic needs, and as they're met, new needs arise in a pyramid hierarchy. Basics such as food, shelter, and clothing come first. Friends, family, and love come closely behind. And once you've got all those pieces in your pocket, you start longing for something more—true mental challenges, a deeper understanding of your life, or some kind of creative and intellectual fulfillment. In a world where society helps us acquire most of our basic needs, that's often what goes missing. Without meeting your higher needs, you feel unfulfilled.

When your basic needs aren't being met, your body sends out signals. You can feel them at every level—from the obvious to the subtle. Back-to-back meetings all day and you skip breakfast and lunch—by 3 P.M. you've got a headache and your stomach is rumbling. When you need water, you feel thirst. When you're overexposed to the cold, you shiver. But loneliness and sadness are signals, too. They're complex psychological processes that get bundled into simple gut feelings to tell you that something is missing. It's hard to know exactly how to respond to them, but they are definitely asking you to react. **Feeling stuck in life is a signal that once again, your routines have taken over and you aren't heading anywhere new. It is time to respond to the action alarm that** is sounding and start moving your life forward again, toward something you think is wonderful.

In exactly the same way, when you are moving in the wrong direction and you don't feel challenged, your body will send you a signal: You will feel stuck. You will feel a distance between you and the world. You will feel checked out, as if you're going through the motions. There is a need that's not being met, and your mind is telling you: *Pay attention! You need to deal with this.* Ignoring the feeling doesn't make it go away—it just creates more problems.

I'm not saying that you need to give up television, but you do need to become your own drill sergeant if you want to reach your dreams. If the hardest choice you made for yourself this week was between Thai or Chinese takeout, you're avoiding challenge at your own expense. You need to take an honest appraisal of the things you're avoiding in your own life, and ask yourself why. If your best response is too lame to pass scrutiny, then it's time to do something about it.

You aren't supposed to be stuck. You are supposed to be doing something amazing with your life. You never know where attacking a true challenge might lead you. But when you do it, whether you succeed right away or not, you discover a new you. A better you. A braver you. A more powerful you. You discover the person you are meant to be.

APPENDIX

I threw a lot at you in this book with one goal in mind—to convince you that the only obstacle in your way is you. I've proven over and over that your brain and your feelings screw you over. You've met dozens of people that kept themselves stuck because they listened to their feelings and their fears. The message is simple: You have the power to stay stuck or to push yourself forward. You have learned a very simple step-by-step method to push yourself and your life in new directions. You have what you need to change your life.

I hope you gained the inspiration and courage to finally step up, push yourself forward, and grab what you deserve from your life.

Whenever you feel off track just flip back to this section for a quick reminder of what we've covered and what you need to do:

Rule #1

Just do the things you don't feel like doing

Remember, your brain and your feelings screw you over when it comes to taking action. They've got a bunch of crafty ways to make you stay stuck.

► *Your Mind Pushes You to Take Anti-Actions*

You know what you need to do. You just busy yourself doing other things instead: surfing the Web, taking a little longer, watching TV, sleeping in, working on something that isn't important, running errands. These are the actions you busy yourself with, instead of the ones you need to take care of. If you find yourself taking anti-actions, it's time to push through.

► *Game Changer vs. Protective Thoughts*

All day long you have "Game Changer" thoughts and you have "Protective Thoughts" that battle them. Your brain is more likely to believe the protective thoughts over the new game-changer ideas. It's called the "Status Quo Bias," and it means that you love the way things are. Your mind will fight against any change in routine. It hates the idea of trying something new.

Always push yourself toward the game-changer thoughts.

► *Feeling Tired Is a Trick*

You are not tired. You just feel tired. You could easily push through, if you forced yourself to. So force yourself to push through fatigue. Fatigue is for chickens and jerks; you are more powerful than that.

Rule #2

You never know where this could lead

Stop overanalyzing. Stop waiting for the right time. Put yourself on a collision course with what you want. You never know where things could lead if you actually forced yourself to push through your fear and go to that meeting, make that phone call, or ask for that favor. If you keep surfing the Web, thinking about it, and waiting for the right time, it won't lead anywhere.

Rule #3

Five-second rule

Whenever you have a game-changer impulse, act on it within five seconds or else it dies. The fastest way to act is to feed that impulse by telling someone your idea and asking for that person's help.

Rule #4

Stop trying to pick, find a way to do both

Stop limiting your life to "either" this "or" that. Always figure out ways to do "both." If you approximate your dreams, you can think "and" not "either/or" and figure out small ways to have everything you want in your life.

Rule #5

Frequency trumps intensity

The rule of thumb you should always follow is frequency over action. If you can only exercise for five minutes today—great, do it. It still counts. If you can only make one phone call—then make one. Stop waiting for large chunks of time and start chunking your actions into smaller bits instead.

Rule #6

If you get rejected, make a new map

When you are powerful, you put a lot of ideas into play. Not all of them are going to win. That means rejections are coming and you'll be tempted to circle the drain of disappointment and get stuck again. As soon as you get rejected, milk sympathy for a couple of hours, then get powerful and create a new map to show you the way forward.

Rule #7

If you feel overwhelmed, do a brain dump

When you are overwhelmed, it's because there is way too much going on in your head. Your brain is fried and spilling over. You need to dump it all out on several pieces of paper. Cross off anything that can be handled later and pick one thing to do. Your head will be clear and getting into action will make you powerful again.

Rule #8

If you just can't motivate yourself—then make it someone else's job

If you just can't get out of bed, or get out the door to run, or get that business plan written, or create that online dating profile— outsource it. Leave yourself no choice. If you get someone else to do it or to police you, you'll actually get it done.

Resources

Most people get stuck when they feel like they've run out of people to talk to, ideas to pursue, or examples to follow. If you find yourself in this camp, try one of my favorite resources or tricks to push yourself forward and take action.

Hire a Coach

I was trained as a life coach by Lauren Zander, who created the Handel Method™. She's the one who first told me I was being a "chicken" and a "brat" about life. She teaches her methodology at MIT, Columbia, and Stanford business schools and has coaches all around the world that will work with you. You can learn more about their coaching, courses, group sessions, and methodology at www .handelgroup.com. If you mention this book, you will receive a special discount on coaching services.

Find a Blog

One of the fastest ways to get yourself connected with like-minded people is through blogs. You can find top blogs on any subject at either www.alltop.com or Google Blog Search. Simply find the top blogs in the categories you are interested in. Join the community, participate in the forums, and subscribe to the RSS feed. You'll immediately start to feel connected and inspired by what you read.

Career Resources

Realmatch is my favorite online resource for career advice, career coaching, and career change. Realmatch will take your skill set and experience and match you with opportunities. There is also a robust career resources section with coaching, articles, ideas, and advice to help you push your career to new heights. Check them out at www .realmatch.com.

Talk to Me Every Day

I'm always here for you. You can follow me on Twitter @melrobbins. Fan me on Facebook. Listen to my radio show at www.mel robbins.com. I update my blog every day and send out newsletters every week. You can also read my monthly column in *Success* magazine. Consider me a friend that is here to help and inspire you. Send me your questions. Tell me what you are up to and how I can help. Everything I write, say, or send out is meant to help you become more powerful in your life.

ACKNOWLEDGMENTS

Hank and Steve. I am the luckiest woman on the planet to have best friends as extraordinary as you two dingbats. Thank you for picking me as your pal and your partner. I was a pain in the ass during this process and so were both of you. You two demand that I be more powerful, always—and because of it this book will change the life of anyone who dares to read it. I love you.

Nena and Jan. Detailing all that you both do would make it sound small. So I won't. You each simply rock.

Rick, Tina, Tammy, Courtney, Meredith, Nate, and the entire team at Crown. Thank you for believing in my ideas and working hard to make them even better. All of you challenged me to write a "smart feast" about being stuck in life and because of that guidance, it actually is. I hope we get to do this again and again and again. Next time, I promise I'll actually deliver chapters.

Mark. You took my circular ADHA repetitive ramblings and turned them into a killer book! You have the perfect wheelhouse of existential philosophy, pop psychology, and entertaining prose. I couldn't have written this without your partnership, your talent, and your friendship and wouldn't have wanted to.

Mom, Dad, and Derek. For always believing that I could do whatever I put my mind to and somehow making sure I knew it, too.

Katie and George. TV and radio is a crazy business, and you two always keep me focused on the bigger picture, especially when things are flatlining.

Stacey. The list is way too long. For all that you do, Chris and I thank you.

To my closest circle of friends. Jonathan. Lisa. Gretchen. Bill. Joanie. Mattie. Nicole. David. Darren. Gwen. Charlie. Jane. Lisa. Robin. Heath. Christine. Dana. Carol. Lisa. Paul. Alison. Dava. Marit. All of you believe in me and make sure I know it. And damn do I appreciate it. I don't say so near enough.

Lauren Zander. You trained me to be a coach over a decade ago, and I am forever grateful. The work you do is changing the world, and I love watching it happen.

Judie. For all those long walks in Vermont where we always conclude *it's all about pushing through fear.*

Lauren, Tracy, and Jani, the amount of work you plow through every day for Hank, Steve, and me is astonishing. I am able to do all that I do because you three have the details and production covered. You're each ah-mazing!

I would also like to thank anyone and everyone who should be on the list. You know who you are.

Last, and most important—Christopher, Sawyer, Kendall, and Oakley. You guys suffer the most as I pursue my passion to help people. Soy, Kdog, and Oaks, you three are patient beyond your years as I jump on conference calls, write for hours, fight with Steve, plaster the walls with my note cards, or hop on a plane, again and again. Your support and belief in me is the greatest gift, and I plan to give each of you the same for the rest of your lives.

Christopher, I love you most.

ABOUT THE AUTHOR

MEL ROBBINS is a married working mother of three, an Ivy-educated recovering criminal lawyer, a rising media star, and one of the top career and relationship experts in America. Widely respected for her grab-'em-by-the-collar advice and tough love, Robbins drills through the mental clutter that stands between people and what they want. Her approach is smart, effective, and entertaining. Five days a week, Mel hosts her own syndicated radio show *The Mel Robbins Show,* discussing hot topics and giving advice to callers across America. She also has a major advice-giving television show in development. In addition, she writes a monthly column for *Success* magazine and is the cofounder of Advice for Living, Inc., which develops products and television programming with experts in the wellness, health, relationship, and career categories.

Most nights, once the kids are in bed, you'll find Mel at home with a bourbon on the rocks and her Australian shepherd at her feet, writing about life, love, and everything else on her award-winning blog, www.melrobbins.com.